Keith Haring's Line

Keith Haring's Line

Race and the Performance of Desire

Ricardo Montez

Duke University Press   Durham and London   2020

Designed by Courtney Leigh Richardson and typeset in Minion Pro
and Helvetica Neue by Copperline Book Services

Library of Congress Cataloging-in-Publication Data
Names: Montez, Ricardo, [date].
Title: Keith Haring's line : race and the performance of desire /
Ricardo Montez.
Description: Durham : Duke University Press, 2020. |
Includes bibliographical references and index.
Identifiers: LCCN 2019050672 (print) | LCCN 2019050673 (ebook) |
ISBN 9781478008606 (hardcover) | ISBN 9781478009535 (paperback) |
ISBN 9781478012191 (ebook)
Subjects: LCSH: Haring, Keith—Criticism and interpretation. |
LA II, 1967– | Jones, Grace. | Goude, Jean-Paul, 1940– |
Muñoz, José Esteban. | Pop art—United States. | Street art— United
States. | Art, American—20th century. | Art and race. Classification:
LCC N6537.H348 M66 2020 (print) |
LCC N6537.H348 (ebook) | DDC 700.92—dc23
LC record available at https://lccn.loc.gov/2019050672
LC ebook record available at https://lccn.loc.gov/2019050673

COVER ART: Tseng Kwong Chi, *Keith Haring body painting
Bill T. Jones*, London, England, 1983. Photo by Tseng Kwong Chi
© Muna Tseng Dance Projects, Inc. www.tsengkwongchi.com.
Art by Keith Haring © The Keith Haring Foundation

This publication is made possible in part with support from
the Barr Ferree Foundation Fund for Publications, Department
of Art and Archaeology, Princeton University.

For José

Lines can be drawn or pulled or written or scribbled or scrawled or, nowadays, be sprayed out of a can. Keith Haring's line is something else. It looks a bit like an engraved line or a sculpted line but it is not either of them. It is a carved line, like the one the man made when he first used it to cut what he wanted out of the air in the back of the cave. **Brion Gysin**, "The Sculpted Line"

Contents

Acknowledgments

Writing from this present, I wish I had begun crafting acknowledgments prior to the book's completion, using it as a means of procrastination in which the litany of support provided by colleagues, friends, family, and institutions might have propelled me to finish this meditation on Keith Haring's life and legacy in a timely manner. Alas, here I am, more than twenty years after the initial impulse to pursue a research project centered on Keith Haring, attempting to recall all those who have made this work possible, an anxiety-producing task with the endless capacity to fill me with a sense of both love and complete dread. Let me get on with it, lest a new wave of writer's block prevent this book from ever materializing. I should begin, then, by thanking Ken Wissoker, whose patience, belief in the project, and editorial guidance were invaluable as I took considerable time to translate a somewhat clumsy Deleuzian project into something more accessible and more reflective of my passion for Haring's complicated line. The anonymous readers provided necessary feedback for revision, and Alison Brown at Henry Street Editing was a master at illuminating a narrative arc that honored my ideas while being attentive to the reviewers' observations. I cannot thank Joshua Tranen enough for his help with the publication process.

This book could not have materialized in its current form without the assistance of the Keith Haring Foundation, especially its director Julia Gruen and creative director Annelise Ream. Additionally, Fawn Krieger, Anna Gurton-Wachter, and Elen Woods assisted me with research at the foundation's office.

My years as a graduate student in the Department of Performance Studies at New York University radically transformed my relationship to visual art and allowed me to understand its performative capacities in new and exciting ways. I am forever grateful to that intellectual space and the challenging conversations that occurred there. The diverse approaches to performance exhibited by Barbara Kirshenblatt-Gimblett, Ann Pellegrini, Peggy Phelan, and Diana Taylor were central to the development of a truly interdisciplinary worldview. Barbara Browning, in particular, understood my project in its infancy—in some ways better than I did. Her expert criticism coupled with her generosity of spirit allowed me to find my way through the material. Fred Moten's tour through Samuel Delany's Neveryon series (conducted under the ruse of a course that purported to trace the anthropological foundations of performance studies) seemed to rewire my brain, changing thought patterns on a synaptic level and allowing me to feel Haring's graphic line as a racial project—a manifestation of history and desire. I continue to learn from those seminar conversations, as ideas downloaded into my consciousness then only now reveal themselves with brilliant clarity. I do not imagine any of us truly grasp the immensity of knowledge that Fred has shared in his writing and conversations. Karen Shimakawa introduced a vitality to the department shortly after I completed coursework. She has been one of the most involved mentors over the years, providing material and psychic support far beyond anything I could have hoped for or deserve. Noel Rodríguez continues to keep the PS ship afloat, and I am grateful for the grace and humor with which he helped me navigate systems of bureaucracy. Beyond ensuring I actually received my degree, he often poked the machine so that food was on the table and rent was paid. Carolyn Dinshaw hired me as managing editor of GLQ during my final years of grad school and has been a continued source of inspiration and support. Likewise, fellow Tex-Mex Josie Saldaña invited me to be part of an emergent program in Latino studies at NYU as a postdoctoral faculty fellow. Her mentorship proved invaluable as I developed a pedagogical practice in race and ethnicity studies and began the process of writing the book manuscript. Lisa Duggan, Faye Ginsburg, Gayatri Gopinath, and Anna McCarthy also offered enthusiastic support throughout my time at NYU.

I benefited from the resources of the Society of Fellows at Princeton. As the Cotsen Postdoctoral Fellow in Race and Ethnicity, I was given remarkable opportunities to further my research and writing. The collegial atmosphere of intellectual debate sparked exciting new directions in my scholarship, and I feel truly blessed for the opportunities to have shared work in progress with esteemed scholars there. I thank Leonard Barkan, Scott Burnham, and Susan Stewart for their generosity and guidance as directors of the program. I cannot express enough thanks for the care with which Mary Harper, as executive director, responded to my work, engaged in extensive conversations beyond the confines of the seminar setting, and helped me navigate environs of privilege to which I had yet to be exposed. I am grateful to Daphne Brooks, Anne Cheng, Bill Gleason, and Valerie Smith, who provided much needed professional guidance. Fellow fellows Lucia Allais and Graham Jones, two of the most brilliant people I could ever hope to know, kept me afloat with their friendship. A generous grant from the Barr Ferree Foundation Fund for Publications through the Department of Art and Archaeology at Princeton supported the book's production.

The faculty and students at the New School for Public Engagement (NSPE) shaped this book in profound ways. Ujju Aggarwall, Anthony Anemone, Laura Aurrichio, Bea Banu, Carolyn Berman, Julia Foulkes, Melissa Friedling, Terri Gordon, Joseph Heathcott, Rachel Heiman, Michelle Materre, Fabio Parasecoli, Gustav Peebles, Claire Potter, Tim Quigley, Lisa Rubin, Joe Salvatore, Marcus Turner, Val Vinokur, Aleksandra Wagner, and Mia White have inspired me in their tireless efforts to imagine a better world through their innovations in education. I am not sure how I would have managed the past several years without the insight and friendship of Tracyann Williams. I am deeply honored to have Danielle Goldman and Soyoung Yoon as coconspirators at Lang. Ted Kerr, a former student who now teaches at NSPE, has been a role model for me in his activist scholarship. He pushed me to work harder in my attempts to make sense of HIV and the history of AIDS, and he offered astute editorial suggestions at different points in the manuscript's development. Kia Labeija arrived in my consciousness as a student in my class The Art of Keith Haring, where she immediately stole the stage. I am convinced she taught the other students much more than I ever could, and she definitely provoked for me new ways of seeing Haring's line.

While my Taurean domestic tendencies drive me to isolation, I hardly feel alone with the friends and family who are integral to the way I navigate and think about art. When visual art was still alienating to me, Catherine Honoré-Jones taught me how to perceive color and light. She is both of those things. John Andrews and I have survived together for what feels like a long time now, and I have been lucky to have his intelligence and humor in my life. My performance studies sisters, Christine Balance and Alexandra Vazquez, keep the beat going and teach me how to navigate vibrational fields with beauty and grace. Patty Ahn, Chad Bennett, Joshua Chambers Letson, Ann Cvetkovich, Cynthia Director, Licia Fiol-Matta, Jonathan Flatley, Joshua Javier Guzmán, Heather Lukes, Molly McGarry, Tavia Nyong'o, Hiram Pérez, Roy Pérez, Sandra Ruiz, Karen Tongson, Eric von Stein, Jeanne Vaccaro, and Shane Vogel have heard me speak about Keith Haring in varying states of sobriety over the years, offering encouragement and inspiration in their critical approaches to aesthetics. The art and performances of D-L Alvarez, Tad Beck, Justin Vivian Bond, Travis Boyer, AA Bronson, Nao Bustamante, Jibz Cameron, Jorge Ignacio Cortiñas, Adriana Corral, Rosson Crow, Vaginal Davis, Benjamin Fredrickson, Sam Green, Erik Hanson, Tom Kalin, Kenny Mellman, Carmelita Tropicana, Ela Troyano, Vincent Valdez, Conrad Ventur, and Matt Wolf have sustained me throughout the writing of this book. These artists, many of whom generously read parts of the manuscript in process, have shown me different ways of being with and in history through their stunning and challenging engagements with the world. Arnaldo Cruz-Malavé, whose book on Juanito Xtravaganza and Keith Haring greatly informs this project, has been an encouraging force within the academy. Jennifer Doyle has gone above and beyond as a true friend and in her professional support. Her scholarship moves me like that of few others, and I continually return to her work as a model of critical analysis in feeling.

Manuel Montez gave me everything he possibly could and then some. While he might not have totally understood what I was up to in New York City, he always made sure I felt his love and was my greatest promoter. Jovita Montez maintains this foundation of support with her love, laughter, and sharp tongue. I have, for better or worse, inherited her entire repertoire of facial expressions, ensuring you will likely know exactly what I am thinking at any given moment. Xochil Arellano and Lisa Montez first introduced me to queer aesthetics, whether they knew it or not.

I never anticipated experiencing so much loss while working on this book structured around loss. Over the past few years, I have been surrounded by an expansive network of friends who have kept me grounded in the process of mourning and have supported me through my more melancholic periods. First and foremost, David Kurnick, who came into my life through old-school cruising on an art house escalator, has held me steady, often trusting my impulses more than I do, giving me the confidence to pursue this project to its completion, and generously working through the manuscript with me. I am thrilled that John and Luann Kurnick and Kate Quiñonez are also part of my family. Matt Brim, Erin Boyle Dempsey, Chloe Edmonson, Laura Gutiérrez, Jodi Hibler, Jared Hohlt, Chad Kia, Heather Love, Joan Lubin, Joshua Lubin-Levy, Michael Miller, Mara Mills, Lindsay Sepulveda, Rachel Saltz, Anamargret Sanchez, David Schliefer, Jake Short, Rebecca Sumner Burgos, Jonathan Taylor, Guinevere Turner, and Hentyle Yapp indulged in all modes of hanging out and kept me sane through life-changing events.

I always thought this book would be inscribed to Keith; I hope my attempts to think through his line convey my deep regard for and fascination with him. Instead, I have dedicated it to José Esteban Muñoz, whose thought and spirit fueled everything in my approach to Keith. José seemed more eager than anyone to see the book realized, and I can only hope that it fulfills a small fraction of what he imagined was possible.

On a Saturday morning in 1983, Arnie Zane filmed his partner, the legendary choreographer and dancer Bill T. Jones, as Keith Haring painted Jones's body, and photographer Tseng Kwong Chi shot some of the most iconic images of all three artists' careers. The video Zane edited from this footage captures an intense performance of interracial exchange in a London studio, where four prominent figures from the creative world of downtown New York interact in a cosmopolitan scene of art production. The video opens with the photo shoot, following Jones's movements under Tseng's direction. Using a still tripod shot, in which Haring and Tseng move between the camera and Jones, Zane keeps his focus on the naked black body of his lover and artistic partner. Each time a flash registers from Tseng's camera, the video cuts to a different pose held by Jones. "Burning Down the House" by Talking Heads is the soundtrack. Quickly, the action jumps backward in time to the preparation of Jones's body for still photography, as we watch Haring carefully painting smooth white lines onto Jones's torso. Jones sits in front of a lighted dressing room mirror, containing his movement, as Haring slowly produces an extensive design across his chest and back. Bodies with upwardly stretched arms, a horned creature, non-representational lines that contour the shape of Jones's body—all are incorporated into a larger spectacle of primitive iconography. With each edit cut, more and more of Jones's black skin is colonized by Haring's hand. While Zane's cuts interrupt the flow of Haring's brushwork, the video still evidences Haring's remarkable skill, his ability to produce a fluid line and create striking outline forms while expertly adjusting the scale of his imagery, moment by moment, to suit his painting surface. Haring creates a line that in its appropriative citation of primitive art can ironically feel unique and original to the artist, particularly given his mesmerizing facility with the brush and his embodied, intimate engagement with a living canvas. The simplicity and immediacy of Haring's work belies his virtuosic skill.

This instance of interaction with live flesh seems to make literal Haring's ability to animate and enliven the many surfaces he encounters. The paint registers those places on Jones's body where Haring has made contact, each brush stroke leaving a visible trace of interracial exchange. Throughout the video, Haring crouches on the edges and in the periphery of the frame; his figure cannot tempt Zane's camera away from its obsessive focus on Jones's body, seen alternately in parts and as a whole. In two consecutive extended shots, Haring paints Jones's butt cheeks and then his inner thighs. In the first of these, Haring brushes a circular spiral pattern on each cheek. While Jones maintains a relative stillness, slight movements of his muscles cause the flesh to shift subtly under Haring's expanding neoprimitive line. The close-ups that follow place Jones's genitalia center stage. Haring makes three strokes over his subject's penis, as if to explain his plan of execution, then proceeds to paint the lower abdomen and thighs. The intimate close-up renders and exaggerates the slightest physical movements; Jones's penis bobs slightly, and his testicles move with his constricted breath. Describing the London photo shoot to Haring biographer John Gruen in an interview published in 1991, Jones states, "Of course, I'm totally naked, and Keith started at the top of me and gradually moved down with the brush, making these incredible patterns. Finally, he reaches my penis, and he does these last three stripes on it. . . . And he looks up at me in that kind of way he has with that little smile of his—and

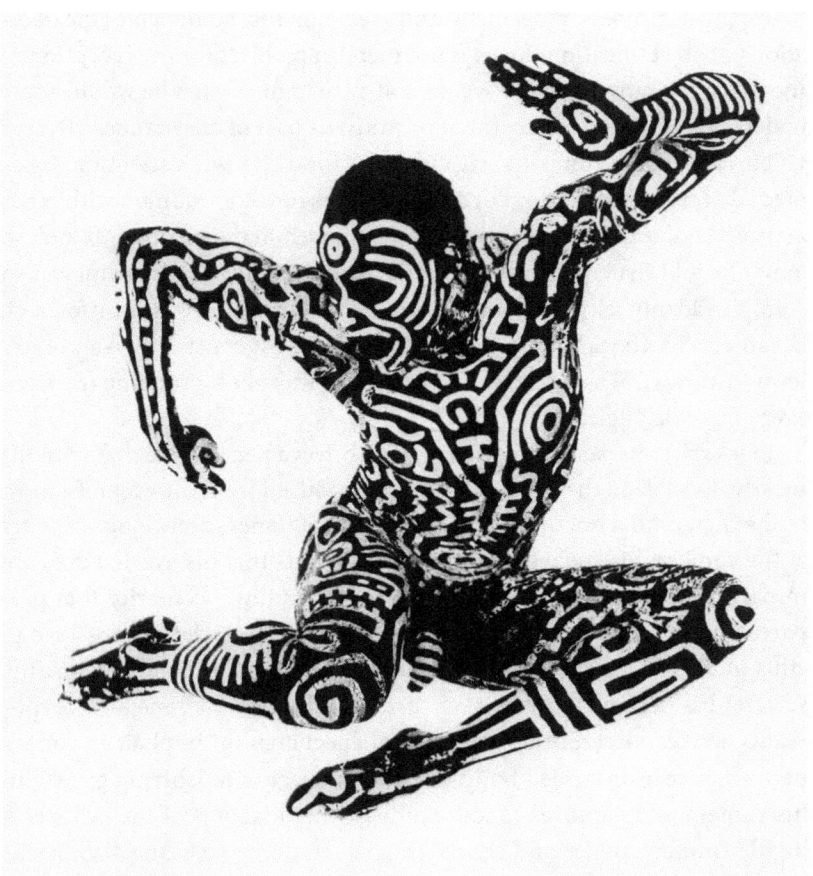

it was total communion at that moment."[1] Zane's video reproduces this unfolding event through a kind of reverse striptease, in which the gradual covering of Jones's body finally reaches the crotch: the grand finale in a scene of erotic spectatorship.

Tseng's printed stills of Jones's painted body, originally produced for Haring's 1983 show at Robert Fraser's London gallery, tend toward an objectification of the choreographer's body, which seems to exist as simply another medium for Haring's line (figure I.1). Zane's video, however, in

---

Figure I.1. Bill T. Jones, body painted by Keith Haring, London, England, 1983. Photo by Tseng Kwong Chi © Muna Tseng Dance Projects, Inc., www.tsengkwongchi.com. Art by Keith Haring © The Keith Haring Foundation.

highlighting process, movement, and spectatorship, complicates the operations of objectification. Jones is not merely an object for the reception of the line but a moving figure whose ability to endure what he would come to describe as a kind of becoming primitive is part of his virtuosity. In the video, Jones's skill competes with Haring's for the viewer's attention. Jones takes direction with expert control and enters into communion with other artists' visions, ultimately transforming himself in the process. "It took so long!" he told Gruen. "Over four hours! And the white acrylic paint was so cold! I suddenly felt what it must be to be a bushman! I was transformed, because as Keith was painting me, I moved almost constantly—and I followed Kwong Chi's instructions, because he was photographing me from every possible angle."[2]

Jones's first-person account of process offers a perspective that remains mostly invisible in the video and photos produced from the event. In most of the images that document the performance, Jones rarely looks directly at the camera; his spoken commentary suggests that his averted eyes are in part a deflection of a colonial gaze, the framing specularity that prepares and consumes his body as neoprimitive spectacle. Where Tseng's stills index Haring's formal versatility—his capacity to fluidly adjust the scale of his designs to fit myriad surfaces—the video's sensuous corporeality makes visceral the processes of spectatorship implicit in Jones's performance as inscribed body. Zane both enacts a fetishizing gaze with his camera and captures Jones's complex mobilization of his skills as a highly trained dancer and choreographer. In doing so, Zane also marks a differentiation between Haring and Jones. The context in which Jones "felt what it must be to be a bushman" is necessarily defined by an erotics of spectatorship and the consumption of otherness in a racially mixed field. Haring's brushwork, Tseng's photography, and Zane's filming are all of course visual engagements with the black body; but of these three, Zane's video—in revealing Jones's body as the focal point around which these other inscribing bodies circulate—gives the best sense of how this economy of visual exchange is performed into being. Zane's video gives us the frame of the performance, staging a naked black body becoming "bushman" via the inscription of paint and of technical capture, even as it also gives us the interplay between the fetish object as canvas and the fetish object as living, vital subject.

This moment of artistic production represents but one scene of cross-racial contact in Keith Haring's brief but phenomenally productive career. Often described as a graffiti artist by virtue of his renegade chalk drawing on New York City subway platforms, Haring became associated with black and Latinx hip-hop culture in the popular imagination. This association was not just a fantasy but also reflected Haring's physical proximity to black and Latinx youth and his work with artists of color in varying contexts. This book critically examines how racial narratives cohere around the artist while exploring Haring's own racial framing of the world. The artist wrote in his journals that he did not feel white on the inside, and he often expressed a fetishistic desire for people of color; in these bodies, he found a soul more akin to his than that of white people. Examining his compulsive draw toward the brown men he serially objectified in an unfulfilled desire to have and be something other than white, *Keith Haring's Line* looks at Haring's racial fantasies but resists a simplistic narrative in which the artist's success is reduced to a white/brown binary of cultural appropriation and exploitation. Through a close reading of Haring's articulations and descriptions of whiteness, the book is attentive to the historical processes of racialization and examines the various ways in which race is reified through often contradictory narratives. Producing a narrative arc that follows the line as it travels across surfaces, from subway walls to canvas to black flesh, the book contextualizes Haring's neoprimitive inscriptions within a modernist tradition of primitivist fantasy; for Haring's line, while often borrowing from graffiti's aesthetic codes, also indexes a graphic history of colonial expansion, the emergence of race as a classifying discourse, and a Western desire for other bodies. I argue that Haring's painted line is a racial project with the capacity both to signify and to animate fields of cross-racial desire.

Though my argument thematically revolves around an idea of Haring's line, the narrative of the book does not follow the traditional linear path of the artist's monograph, resisting a teleological heroic narrative of the artist in favor of a performative engagement with the traces of Haring's life. These include standard biographical materials, such as artworks, published interviews, and photographs that document Haring's existence, but this evidence acts as an animating force, which provokes detours into the lives and works of other cultural producers who form a constellation within a larger field of cross-racial contact and queer desire. While the book addresses dynamics of race and desire that have been largely undertheorized in the critical reception of Haring's art, I do not uncover some previously unseen or unknowable truth about the artist, rewriting his biography according to a more correct version of events (most of what I analyze has been widely accessible). This would betray my sense of Haring's line and obscure the potentialities in the unresolved nature of queer desire. The complicity between cultural producers that I elaborate in the following section extends to my own role as a critic as I attempt to theorize an understanding of Haring's art through my own relationship to the material. Given the influence of Roland Barthes on both Haring's artistic imagination and my own analysis, I take inspiration from D. A. Miller's *Bringing Out Roland Barthes*, in which the literary critic writes through and across the gay sexuality he shares with the deceased Barthes, an exercise that Miller understands to be informed by fantasy and projection. Referring to a produced knowledge of Barthes's sexuality, Miller writes, "What I most sought, or what I most seek now in the evidence of Roland Barthes's gayness is the opportunity it affords for staging this imaginary relation between us, between those lines on which we each in writing them may be thought to have put our bodies—for fashioning thus an intimacy with the writer whom (above all when it comes to writing) I otherwise can't touch."[3] Like Miller's approach to Barthes, this book on Haring might be understood as "an album of moments" in which I respond to names, artworks, and archival matter to produce an idea of the artist conditioned by my affective relations to him. Through the provocations of Haring's journals, I enact in these pages a kind of biographical image that resists objective representation in favor of a different type of portrait that might more effectively speak to the ambivalent nature of cross-racial desire, the animating capacities of Haring's line, and the emotional vicissitudes of an embodied, which is to say felt, knowledge that cannot be proved in any absolute sense.

This methodological orientation applies as well to the uncontained nature of that which I describe as the archive. While later in this introduction, I locate myself as a researcher in the Warhol Museum, referring to a collection of Polaroids protected within physical and administrative structures, the archive that animates this project exceeds these walls (and those of the Keith Haring Foundation), as I constitute a larger assemblage of materials, ephemera, and feelings related to the artist. Taking inspiration from a seminal text on the performative capacity of archival materials, this book reflects what Ann Cvetkovich describes as "an 'archive of feelings,' an exploration of cultural texts as repositories of feelings and emotions, which are encoded not only in the content of the texts themselves but in the practices that surround their production and reception."[4] As such, the book performs against the tradition of the artist's monograph; I follow connective threads into the lives and work of other figures, departing at times from a tight focus on Haring to convey something of the vitalizing capacity of his art and the energizing residue of his contact with the world. And, like Cvetkovich, I am feeling my way through materials left in the wake of traumatic loss associated with AIDS.

Collaboration and Complicity in the Scene of Racial Production

I open with the scene of artistic exchange in London because it speaks to this book's larger concerns about Haring's inspirational contact with other bodies and the effects his success had on the lives and visibility of those with whom he worked. Jones's description and Zane's video draw out the activity behind the photograph, a still document in which Haring's vibrant white inscriptions on the form of a black male body threaten to overshadow the participation of others in this scene. Circulating in a world conditioned by a graphic history of white male domination, Tseng's photographs of Jones necessarily risk reproducing a violating objectification of the black body, highlighting the mastery of the white male artist over the virtuosity of those others who are indispensable to the art's creation. One could follow this line of thinking across all of Haring's art production, in its citation and appropriation of graphic sign systems that are inextricably bound to the expressive visual cultures of nonwhite subjects.[5] To do so, however, would be to reproduce fixed relationships among reified ideas of race, culture, and power. Resisting the piously seductive critique of Haring's appropriative and exploitative practices, this book pays particular attention to the line in Haring's art as a mobile sign that, while indexical of violent histories of contact with bodies of color, also imbues surfaces with a constantly animating force, producing meaning and experiences that exceed any fixed representation of history.

As I discuss in chapter 1, "Desire in Transit: Writing it Out in New York City," Haring develops a painting-as-writing practice inspired by an education in semiotic theory and the "magical" writing practices of queer artists like William Burroughs and Brion Gysin. That chapter explores how Haring's iconography emerged from his study of sign systems and the performative capacity of visual vocabularies. Working in the conceptual spaces between aurality, visuality, and signification, Haring experimented across media platforms while a student at New York's School of Visual Arts from 1978 to 1980. I argue that Haring's activity during his time at SVA, which included video art and performance as well as painting, laid the groundwork for his visual style and the modes of public art performance that came to define his career. New to the city, Haring was not only exposed to an invigorating world of ideas and intellectual exchange, he was also immersed in a field of contact with new bodies and new opportunities for the exploration of his desire. This book argues that the development of his line, in its signifying potential, was inextricably bound to a field of, and education in, cross-racial desire.

If Bill T. Jones understands some of the potential repercussions of Haring's line as it appears on his black body, he also registers the line's relationship to Haring's personal life. Jones tells Gruen about the affinity he had for Haring who, like him, had grown up as a "country boy" (Haring was raised in central Pennsylvania, Jones in upstate New York) and only later became accustomed to the pretensions of bourgeois city life. Jones also felt a connection because of their involvement in interracial relationships. Arnie Zane, Jewish and middle class, was instrumental in Jones's development from country boy to city artist. Jones found in Zane an encouraging companion, who helped him overcome the insecurity he experienced in the early days of their relationship. In the interview with Gruen, Jones recalled that "at the beginning, I felt my inadequacies. I mean, I couldn't balance a checkbook. And people wouldn't even talk to me, because they assumed Arnie had the brains. But he was the one who encouraged me and promoted me."[6] It is significant that Jones, when asked to elaborate on his relationship with Haring, circles back to his own life with Zane, in a kind of sideways approach to the question of Haring's impulse toward cross-class relationships with men of color. This was an impulse that Jones clearly understood and just as clearly felt ambivalent about. As the interview with Gruen continues, Jones says he attempted to talk to Haring, with mixed results, about the obligations one incurs in undertaking intimate relations with men of differing class and race. "What I'm trying to say is that Keith loves people from a class lower than his own. Well, there's a responsibility that goes with that. And that responsibility is not just how generous you are but how you can bring that person up through his emotional perils and feelings of inadequacy." Jones claims that while Haring cared for his lovers, he never fully examined the repercussions of his interracial relationships and, in fact, retreated the more he was pushed on the subject; in particular, Jones explains that Haring failed to consider the difficult situation in which his lovers might find themselves in the racist and classist art world. Rather than calling Haring a racist, Jones argues, "He doesn't understand that he is a product of a racist environment."[7]

What does it mean for Jones to understand Haring, and implicitly himself, as products of a racist environment? Accepting Haring's line on his body and enabling Tseng and other photographers to distribute signifying documents laden with a history of colonial contact, Jones might easily be understood as colluding in a scene of racist fantasy, in a process akin to that explicated by Kobena Mercer (in his well-known discussion of Robert Mapplethorpe's photographs) by which "elements of commonplace racial stereotypes . . . regulate, organize, prop up and *fix* the process of erotic/aesthetic objectification in which the black man's skin becomes burdened with the task of symbolizing the transgressive fantasies and desires of the white gay male subject."[8] The charge can hardly be denied; but, as Mercer's emphasis here on fixity indicates, this way of phrasing the point also assumes that the script is already written, a dead letter that the bodies in play do no more than animate.[9] The scene Jones describes might instead be understood as a collaborative moment in which each artist uses a talent necessary to the conditions of production. The imagery that Tseng produced with Haring is often seen as archival documentary evidence of Haring's world, a kind of supplementary photojournalistic record of the artist's life. As the sole surviving figure from the London photo shoot (the interview with Gruen was published in 1991; Haring and Tseng had died in 1990, Zane in 1988), Jones underscores Tseng's contributions and, in doing so, to some degree destabilizes the prominence that Haring's work holds in the images. Explicitly naming the photographer's work as integral to his own performance for the camera, Jones makes visible a participatory labor that might go unnoticed by those who see Tseng's stills merely as documentary proof of Haring's process. The art world's fetishization of Haring's celebrated line, Jones's photographic inscription as an available black body, and the promise of Tseng's photos as indexical representations of the event are simultaneous effects of the imagery that make each artist legible and potentially obscure the interactive dynamics described by Jones.

Collaboration might seem an ideal way to conceptualize this scene, mitigating how Haring's art production overshadows the activity of Tseng and Jones. But the promise of collaboration as a descriptive framework that stresses dialogue and exchange rather than the mastery of a single artist quickly fades when faced with the reality of the art's reception. Collaboration cannot ultimately remake the social world of privilege that values Haring over those with whom he worked. My thinking about the false promise of "collaboration" takes inspiration from decades-long discussions in the discipline of anthropology, where researchers must confront the entanglement of their practice with the legacy of colonialism. As anthropologists came to critique their discipline's romanticization of fieldwork, the ideal of collaboration—supposedly indicating a more egalitarian, polyvocal working relationship between ethnographers and their subjects of study—came to be supplanted by the admission of complicity. George Marcus, in "The Uses of Complicity in the Changing Mise-en-Scène of Anthropological Fieldwork," traces this shift before going on to challenge the notion that researchers can rest once they have acknowledged their complicity with regimes of colonial power. For Marcus, the ethical critique of the power imbalance between ethnographer and subject is revealed as insufficient in a world that cannot be defined through clearly demarcated localities, pure cultural origins, or fixed positions of authority. Citing the *Oxford English Dictionary*'s definition of complicity as a "state of being complex or involved," Marcus forwards an understanding of the term as that which renders impossible the notion that bounded localized cultures can be accessed and known. Complicity as a primary condition of fieldwork, argues Marcus, "is an affinity, marking equivalence, between fieldworker and informant." It is an "acknowledged fascination between anthropologist and informant regarding the outside 'world' that the anthropologist is specifically materializing through the travels and trajectory of her multi-sited agenda."[10] The complicity Marcus describes here moves beyond the idea that the ethnographer's complicity within larger structures of global power simply corrupts any attempt at rapport or collaboration. Instead, it "is both more generative and more ambiguous morally; it demands a mapping onto and entry of the ethnographic project into a broader context that is neither so morally nor cognitively determined."[11]

In this book, I think through complicity as an alternative framework to collaboration within the world and work of Keith Haring. Haring's line, I argue, is an emblem of complicity in the terms outlined by Marcus. It indexes a history of colonialism and appropriation in its citation of primitive art from across the globe, and this appropriation—one that extends to the graffiti practices of black and Latinx youth—can be seen as generative and symptomatic of Haring's erotic and social attraction to people of color. Yet, to make this broad connection between a global history of white domination, Haring's neoprimitive line production, and his libidinal drives—shaped as they are by racial categories of difference—is to impose a story on the line that, while not untrue, potentially encases its mobility within a predictable moral and ethical narrative.

The opening scene of this book—which introduces a set of conditions that resonate across the field of Haring's art production—demands to be read in terms that exceed such fixity. Jones recognizes that he cannot free himself from the limiting conditions of visibility in his partnership with Haring; as he puts it in the conversation with Gruen, he knows that one possible effect of Haring's line is to turn him into "just another black dude." But he also actively performs within the signifying logic of the line, recoding himself in the act of recollection through a discourse of becoming bushman. Like the complicit ethnographer and his informants, bound in a fascination that produces an orientation to the external world, Haring, Jones, Tseng, and Zane are mutually engaging with a sign system of primitive inscription. Within the London studio, they are complicit, manufacturing images in relation to a continually reconstituted and reimagined elsewhere—those spaces of reception in which the images circulate and those geographies that are part of the multiple and shared histories that shape them as subjects. *Keith Haring's Line* frames Haring's relationships as scenes of complicity rather than ones of collaboration in an attempt to stress the dynamic uncertainty of intimate and creative exchange. Echoing Amber Jamilla Musser's privileging of complicity over subversion in her recent analysis of scenes of masochistic play, I understand Haring's neoprimitive line as a graphic enactment, a visual-aesthetic performative, that conjures and draws subjects into a field of negotiations in which the outcome of participation and the agential terms of the subject cannot be forecast according to a perceived power imbalance or structural inequality.[12] Like Musser, I am interested in thinking through flesh as a sensational field through which difference is continually elaborated in an ongoing reorientation to bodily experience.

The problem of recognition in a field of erotic cross-racial spectatorship that arises in Jones's account of his work with Haring resurfaces in each of this book's chapters, as I trace the eruption of Haring's line as the bearer of fantasies of cross-racial access and desire. While chapter 1 sets Haring's early days of erotic exploration in New York City against his developing art practice and his theoretical reflections, chapter 2, "'Trade' Marks: LA II and a Queer Economy of Exchange," explores the erotic dimensions of Haring's fascination with graffiti art, and the complexities of his collaborations with the graffiti artist Angel Ortiz, better known by his tag LA II (or sometimes LA 2). This chapter employs the gay-slang concept of "trade" to explore the financial and affective complexities of Haring's collaborative work. In my usage, "trade" at once designates a severe structural imbalance of power (the racist underpinnings of the art market means that LA II does not necessarily benefit from the ongoing circulation of those pieces he completed with Haring) and evokes how Haring and LA II's work makes those imbalances a source of performative energy: thus "trade" also points to a real affective transaction as well as to a situation of exploitation. Related questions arise in chapter 3, which treats the superstar diva Grace Jones. Jones made her body available for Haring's inscription, provoking art historian Robert Farris Thompson to describe her as "theory made flesh," the corporeal manifestation of all that might be signified by and indexed in Haring's graphic line. In chapter 3, "Theory Made Flesh?: Keeping Up with Grace Jones," I contextualize this fantasy of embodiment within Jones's larger career and previous scenes of complicity with her artistic partner and lover, the French graphic designer Jean-Paul Goude, who claims responsibility for creating "the Grace Jones myth." Rather than presume that Jones simply embodies the possibilities written out for her, I think through Jones's flesh as a site of tension that, through its very availability, paradoxically announces her unknowability. This opacity, the inability to identify a coherent, stable subject, is an inherent quality of every figure—alive and dead—that populates the life of Keith Haring.

Icon and Fetish

A chemical reaction occurred. Andy Warhol pressed the button of his Polaroid, producing a flash and exposing gelatin silver to the light emanating, reflecting, and radiating from Keith Haring and Juan Dubose, his first significant lover (figure I.2). Their forms were caught, written out against a light-sensitive surface. Breathing, living beings, Haring and Dubose existed for Warhol, posing in their desire—allowing themselves to be captured by the artist whose capture brought with it inclusion in a glamorous world of socialites and celebrities. Haring and "his black boyfriend" (as Warhol would refer to Dubose in his diary) are doubly written into a particular existence through the writing of light in the Polaroids and the transcription of a journal entry. Both documents would find their audience in mass production.

The Polaroids were enlarged, the images rewritten in black and white on acetate as positive proofs. The acetate allowed for another light pro-

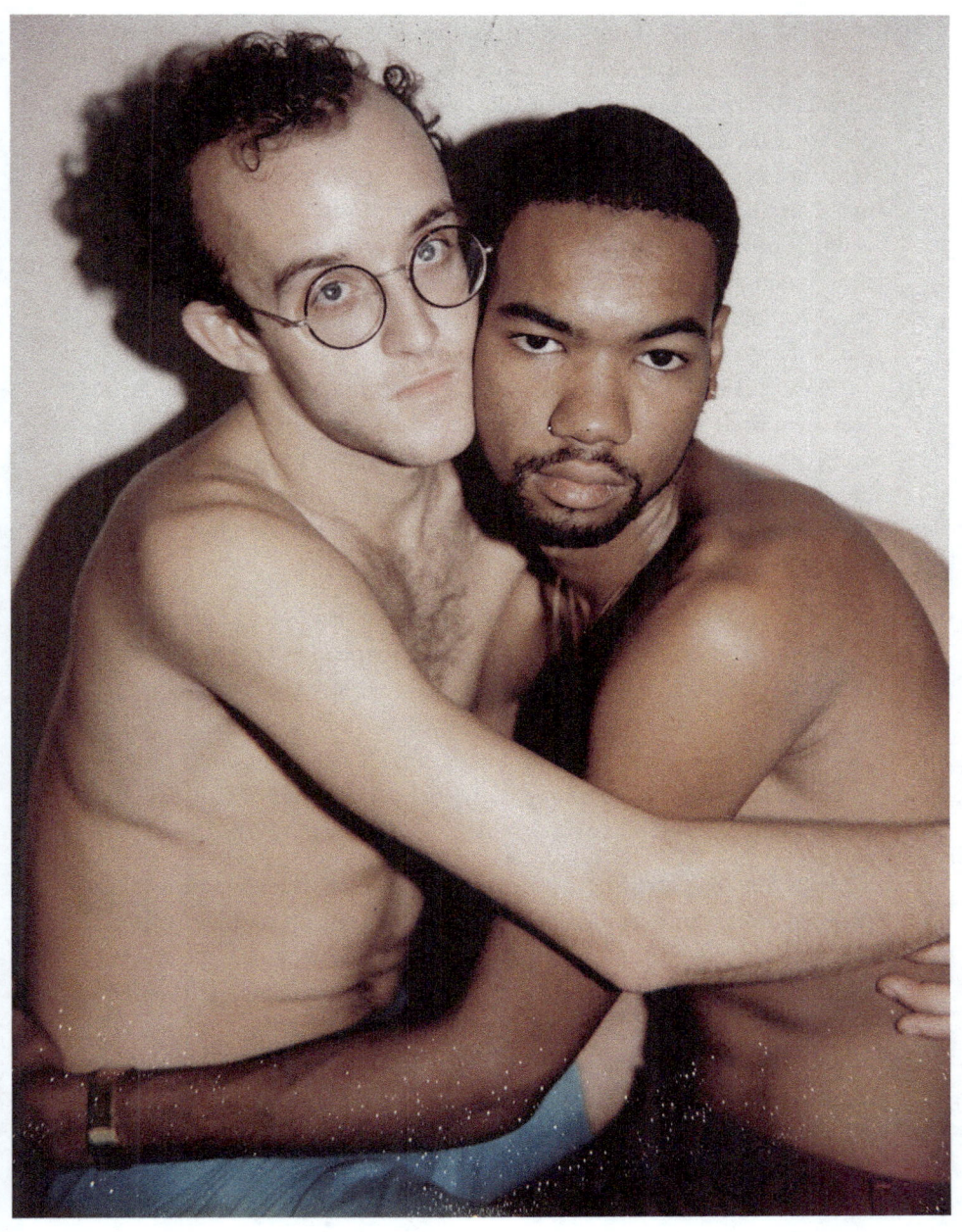

Figure I.2. Andy Warhol, *Keith Haring and Juan Dubose*, 1983. Polacolor ER, 4¼ × 3⅜ inches. © 1983. The Andy Warhol Foundation for the Visual Arts, Inc. / Licensed by Artists Rights Society (ARS), New York.

cess. The silkscreen filter was created when the emulsion was exposed to intense UV light; bright light shot through the acetate, hardening the chemical in those places where exposure occurred. The dark forms on the acetate resisted the passing of light. Washing the emulsion surface, those areas not exposed to light flowed away, leaving a screen image of the lovers. The silkscreen frame used a filter made of silk, or a synthetic material that mimics the single filament thread produced from the silkworm's mouth. Single filament material allows ink to flow smoothly onto the canvas. And so the images of Haring and Dubose were written, rewritten, and painted onto the canvas surface.

The effect is all the more powerful because this particular relationship can seem itself already written—scripted to fit a familiar story about race and power. Dubose's presence in Haring's life seems to follow an overly coherent narrative script. In Gruen's biography, Haring discusses his relationship with Dubose and in the process claims that he is most comfortable in his intimacy with people of color:

> My spirit and soul is much closer to the spirit and soul of people of color. And, yes, I have an erotic attraction for people of color, because there is no better way to be wholly a part of the experience than to be sexually involved. I firmly believe that a sexual relationship—a deep sexual relationship—is a way of truly experiencing another person—and really *becoming* that other person. So I had that with Juan Dubose, who was a black person. And I became part of his life.[13]

Those in Haring's social network often comment on the ever-present dark-skinned boys who occupied his life, and Dubose stands at the origin of this pattern. He exists as a site of becoming for Haring in this anecdote, which explicitly ties erotic intimacy to the artist's racialized sense of self. In chapter 1, I frame this particular erotic fantasy within a larger field of cross-racial desire, in which Haring claims a nonwhite interiority. I discuss how Haring's sexual and professional engagements with people of color were a stimulus for artistic production and personal fantasy throughout his adult life. His fetishization marked people of color as a potential source of freedom from whiteness and the violent histories of subjection that white people have perpetuated; Haring's own complicity with this historical framework remained relatively unproblematized, as he figured his inner "spirit and soul" as different from those of other white people. Haring's liberal presumption to know the inner life of brown people and to imagine his contact with people of color as a means to become nonwhite reveals the context in which Dubose gets marked as a fetish.

Precisely as a fetish, Dubose's place in Haring's life seems overly narratable, even tritely predictable. Exhausted from tooling around the baths and by his failure to meet anyone with whom he could connect beyond sex, Haring reported his 1981 encounter with Dubose in rapturous, expectant terms, and his words conjure Dubose on a purely aesthetic level. "He's black, he's thin, he's the same height as me, and he's almost the same age."[14] After great sex, Haring claimed this black double as "the right person." Dubose wrote his number on stationery from the St. Mark's Baths, and so began Haring's descent into love. A car-stereo installer and DJ, Dubose enters the narrative of Haring's life through the recollection of others. Praised for his quiet beauty and cooking skills, Dubose oscillates between the roles of sexual object and domestic caretaker. Samantha McEwan, who shared an apartment with the couple, told Gruen that Dubose was "the quietest, the most unassuming, beautiful, gentlest, and really mysterious guy."[15] But her tone changes as she recounts the later years of the relationship. The creator of "wonderful meals" becomes a "monosyllabic" drug user who does little more than watch television. McEwan describes an increasingly introverted figure, an inverse image of Haring's increased productivity. "Keith was getting more and more active, Juan just retreated into himself—and it was a very sad thing to watch."[16] Frustrated with Dubose's jealousy and supposed inactivity, Haring eventually left Dubose and began a relationship almost immediately with a Puerto Rican man, Juan Rivera, who remained Haring's lover for several years. Years after the separation from Dubose, Haring received a call from Dubose's mother informing him that his former lover was dying. Haring visited Dubose in the hospital, trying to ensure that he was being treated appropriately for HIV infection. Dubose passed away shortly after the visit, and Haring proceeded to get people to come to the wake in Harlem. Haring recorded in his journals the difficulty he had telling his friends that Dubose had died, writing that it felt like the equivalent of announcing his own death. At the wake, Haring's fears of the open casket were assuaged when he glimpsed Dubose and was able to reassure himself that "he looks so beautiful!"[17]

In Haring's authorized biography and published journals, Dubose's entrance and exit neatly confine him to a secondary timeline to that of his more prolific and famous lover. As an artist, Haring engaged Dubose's fleshly existence in part as a way to further his own racialized fantasy of interior actualization, repeatedly articulating the terms of Dubose's presence within the structure of his own fame. Haring's friends, too, paint a portrait of Dubose that is clearly wedded to and filtered through Haring's desire and his career. Warhol's diaries, which discuss the remarkable photoshoot with Dubose in some detail, do the same. In an entry dated August 18, 1983, Warhol states that "Keith Haring came by with his black boyfriend and I took pictures. They were so lovey-dovey in the photos, it was nutty to see."[18] By the time Haring posed for Warhol, he was rapidly becoming part of the glamorous world of icons Warhol had been documenting and reproducing for years. He fit perfectly in the collection of stars and fashionable figures who populated scenes of excess, wealth, and beauty—a rendering of exclusivity and performed exception that mimicked the counter-cultural, self-produced importance of Warhol's Factory days. Haring's increasing fame and the ubiquity of his work would soon generate a publicity machine that would insert his face and art into the everyday lives of millions around the world. As Rene Ricard had predicted in a 1981 piece in *Artforum*, "Keith Haring" would become a trademarked sign in circulation.[19]

Haring's inclusion in Warhol's stable of subjects both signals Haring's arrival as famous and expedites his production as an icon. In the Warholian context, the generation of multiple canvases with a silkscreen of Haring's image makes perfect sense, but what about the "black boyfriend"? Neither ever-present commodity nor media superstar, Juan Dubose might appear a curious subject for Warhol's reproduction of the period. But the Polaroids from which the silkscreens are produced document and generate a defining relationship for Haring. The scene of bare-chested embrace enabled a series of iconic stills—temporal freezes that index Haring's notion of becoming other through his intimacy with a black man. Warhol's production machine does not seize Juan Dubose as subject in his own right but rather mobilizes his fleshly proximity to Haring to cement the artist's public image as a lover of dark men. Warhol as artist uses Dubose to codify Haring socially. Only within the context of the reproducibility of Haring's cross-racial relations does Dubose become an ideal subject for pop reproduction.

As a researcher invested in the operations of racism and the ways in which subjects are eclipsed or diminished in the story of Haring's life, I have produced a predictable narrative for Dubose and his historical treatment. To research Juan Dubose in the readily available sources on Haring's life is to witness the production of a brown and black sign that is an amalgamation of projections. A direct citation of Dubose's voice appears to be absent from the record. One might seek to somehow recover his voice through his own recorded history or the stories of others who knew him—and thereby to return to Dubose some of the agency and participatory and innovative complicity with racial fantasy that I have attributed to collaborators like Tseng Kwong Chi and Bill T. Jones. But I am interested in Dubose as a counterpoint to the other figures in this book. The absence of his voice and the difficulty in locating alternative representations of him generates a productive resistance to the fantasy of a complete and correct narrative.

The power of that fantasy, and its dangers, have been sensitively analyzed by Arnaldo Cruz-Malavé in a 2007 book that provided a groundbreaking discussion of racial difference in Haring's life and work. In *Queer Latino Testimonio, Keith Haring, and Juanito Xtravaganza*, Cruz-Malavé documents the oral history of Juan Rivera, the man who followed Dubose as Haring's lover. Cruz-Malavé's book presents a direct transcript of recorded interviews with Rivera along with a separate chapter examining Haring's life and success through the lens of racial politics. Cruz-Malavé describes his concern about the possible consequences of sharing Rivera's story with an audience that might be all too eager to consume the sensational tale of a down-and-out Puerto Rican. Entrusted by Rivera, who felt scorned by Haring's authorized biographer, with the task of telling his side of the story, Cruz-Malavé asks, "What if I was providing someone with a walk on the wild side so that someone, me included, could finally feel, could *com-probar*, both confirm and taste that joyous sigh of relief, that jolt that may be experienced at living 'lesser' lives at a distance?"[20] In presenting this scene of complicity, Cruz-Malavé demonstrates that the disenfranchised subject cannot free himself from the economy of desire that denies his agency or commits violence against him. In other words, the recovered voice that would finally set right the historical record can never be more than a fantasy.

On a trip to Pittsburgh in 2005, that fantasy took a different form when I encountered Haring and Dubose—or rather, the imagistic trace of them. After years of researching Haring and writing about the role of cross-racial desire in the production and consumption of his work, my own desires were suddenly reinvigorated on seeing the Polaroids and acetate proofs filed in the collection of ephemera housed in the Andy Warhol Museum. I had seen reproductions of the silkscreen paintings Warhol produced from the photos, but the intensity of these recorded moments of contact, caught on the glossy surfaces of archived Polaroids, hit me viscerally. These scenes of radiant intimacy jarred me in their emotional force. The images display the lovers in a bare-chested embrace. In some shots, their lips touch. In others, they simply stare at the camera. What I had previously experienced as beautiful but cool abstractions on canvas became something altogether different in my contact with this primary material. In the minutes when I first came upon the photos, I wanted to strip off my white archive gloves and pull the images from their plastic casing to expose them as much as I possibly could. I wanted to feel my way into them by touching the material register of light, sensually engaging the photosensitive surfaces that had been in such close proximity to the lovers.[21] Confronted with these Polaroids—images vibrating with the interracial contact that had become the focus of my academic project—I found myself in that fortunate but tricky space where new associations were being made, but their importance refused narrative coherence. Dubose cannot be rescued from the scripts of race and power that frame his story, and those scripts were of course in play in the creation of the Warhol photoshoot; but the intimacy of the light writing in those images made that impossibility seem newly, productively disorienting. Inspired by Jennifer Doyle's *Hold It against Me: Difficulty and Emotion in Contemporary Art*, I am drawn toward experiences of disorientation over fixity as they generate an affective space of criticism that retains the complicated, performative impact of art.[22] In writing *Keith Haring's Line*, the unknowability of my subject has exacerbated a fetishistic relationship to the queer artist and fueled a desire for contact with the traces of Haring's life. *Keith Haring's Line* is written in acknowledgment of that desire and of that frustration, and it explores in particular how the impossible desire for the archive upsets the coherence of biographical narrative.

Against the Heteroheroic Timeline

This book in many ways maps my attempt to respond to an emotional call from archival matter. It indulges an intense contact with this material in order to excavate a queer futurity, a political possibility that vibrates in the records of Haring's past. Warhol's Polaroids, with their suggestion of immediacy, instant capture and development, energize the fetish objects of the archive with the promise and hope of intimacy, an approximation to being there, to having been there. They also heighten my frustrations with the standard narrative that has come to represent the remarkable life of Keith Haring, and they allow me to access the something else of the archive.[23] In other words, the sensorial, affective experience of my own long-ing disrupts the fixed conceptions of who the artist was and what kind of effects his art had and continues to have on the world.

A short sketch of the artist's life as it appears in catalogs and exhibition materials illuminates a standardized narrative. Keith Haring was born on May 4, 1958, in Reading, Pennsylvania, and grew up in nearby Kutztown. Under the tutelage of his father, Haring developed a drawing style in his youth that referenced popular comics and cartoons. In the late 1970s, Har-ing went to art school in Pittsburgh and eventually enrolled in the School of Visual Arts in New York City. Beginning in 1978, Haring was active in a developing downtown art scene that brought together visual art, video, and performance. His art school training, highly informed by semiotic theory, shaped Haring's line form production. By 1980, Haring was tag-ging the city with the chalk outline forms that would eventually garner him wide acclaim as a popular artist and bring him into the spotlight as an art gallery superstar. New York City—a playground of drugs, sex, and endless movement—offered a pulsating energy that fed Haring's art production throughout the 1980s. He devoted much of his time to public works and displayed a commitment to children through his outreach as an artist. While keeping strong social ties to "the street," Haring enjoyed the high life of celebrity, befriending the most fabulous of 1980s icons. In 1988, Haring was diagnosed with HIV, and he died from AIDS-related causes in February 1990, at the age of thirty-one. His foundation continues Haring's legacy of funding for children's and AIDS-related organizations.

This narrative represents one that I have struggled with for almost two decades, as I attempt to reimagine Haring's life outside a standard time-line. Beginnings, ends, and the causal links that join them have produced much anxiety in each of my attempts to map a narrative of Haring's life. Perhaps my critical tale is best understood as beginning in the summer of 1997, when I visited the first full-scale retrospective of the artist at the Whitney Museum of American Art. The exhibit was sequenced accord-ing to a clear—overly clear—biographical telos: the museum's spaces had been configured to lead visitors sequentially through rooms that first in-voked a sunny childhood and then beckoned them into the dark passages of subway tunnels and a glowing and thumping dance space, before termi-nating in a narrow black passage at the end of which, dimly lit by a single bulb, was visible an image of a sperm with horns (figure I.3). The spatial-ized sense of inevitability—of innocence lost to the city, of pleasure suc-cumbing to a sexual plague—was palpable.

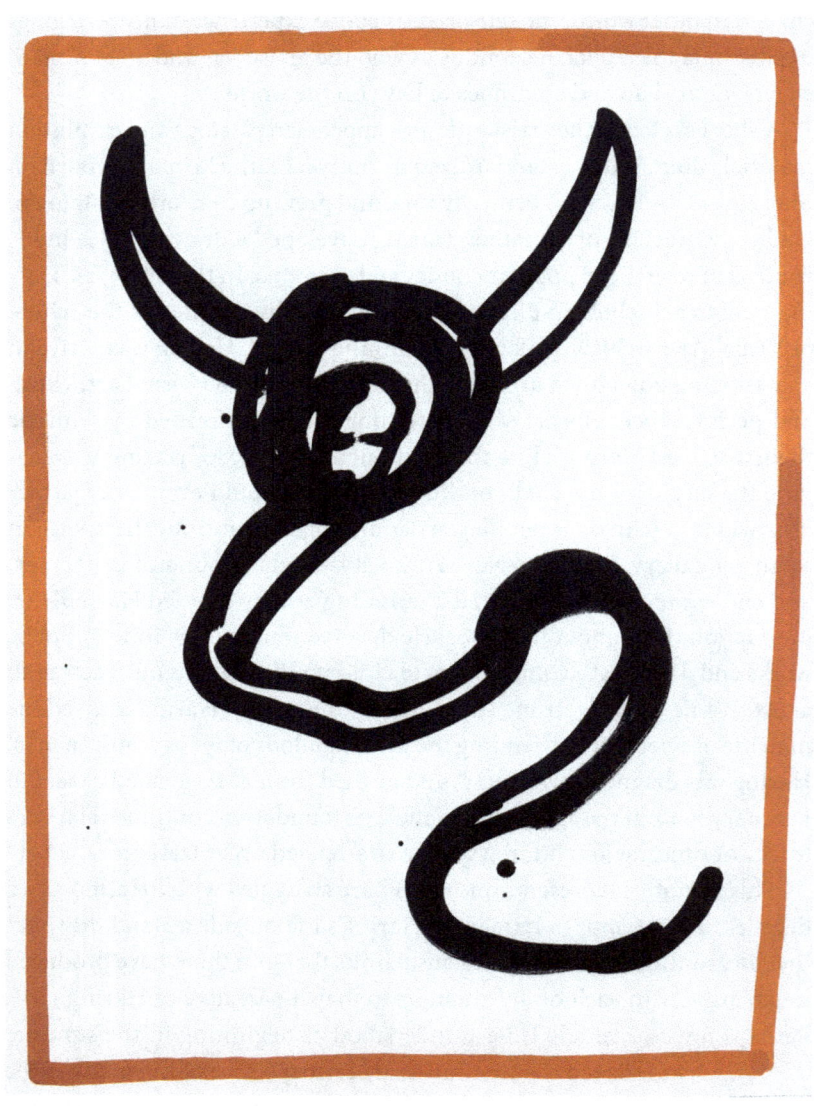

Figure I.3. Keith Haring, *Untitled*, 1988. Sumi ink on paper, 30 × 22 ½ inches.
Art by Keith Haring © The Keith Haring Foundation.

Months before attending the retrospective, I had read Haring's recently published journals. A complex portrait of the artist emerges in these pages, in which written meditations move seamlessly from Roland Barthes to bathhouse sex to considerations of the graphic line. The entries are of course ordered chronologically, but in a potent sense, they defy order; the topics remained independent, jumbled, fragmentary, animated. At the age of twenty-one, I felt hailed by the journals as I prepared for my own move to New York City. The Whitney retrospective seemed perfectly timed for my arrival. Days after moving to the city, I found myself in the presence of Haring's art—and in the presence of some of the actual journal pages on which he wrote: these too had been included in the show. The exhibition's wall text explained the structure of the show, with emphasis on the play the curators wanted to establish between individual art pieces and the ephemera encased in vitrines. The following passage accompanied the exhibit's first vitrine:

> Keith Haring was dedicated to making his art available to the public and his life was linked to his art. As a boy, he used drawing as a form of writing and images as a way of telling a story. The images in this exhibition tell the story of his life; they are, on one level, like a diary. The biographical gaps between images are here filled in by the objects in the vitrines. These are taken from the collections of miscellaneous, often ephemeral things that Haring gathered and that were kept after his death, including photographs, ads, invitations, and old art school projects and assignments. What distinguishes Haring is the seamless exchange between his art and his life. By combining these collections and the art works, the public and the private, this installation presents the visual narrative of a creative life.[24]

In this text, written by curator Elizabeth Sussman and exhibit designers Tibor Kalman and Richard Pandiscio, Haring's art becomes synonymous with his life. His works, conceived of as diary entries, are framed here implicitly to convey a biographical narrative. The ephemera in the vitrines then become objects that fetishistically provide the narrative connections, the biographical integument, between pieces of art. To describe canvases as fragments of life and ephemera as narrative objects sets the stage for a very particular kind of storytelling, in which the presentation of Haring's life ghosts the biological body of the artist. This is the structure of many museum exhibitions, but the curators of Haring's retrospective clearly felt compelled to make explicit the manner in which objects perform. I had responded powerfully to the journals, and I was no less affected by much of the ephemera, which the curators had taken pains to present more or less as journal entries. I left the show in tears.

These tears were in many ways a result of the exhibit's dramatic structure: the objects powerfully conjured Haring's absent presence, but the forceful and preordained directionality of their presentation robbed them of something of their potentiality. My tears were indicative not of cathartic mourning but of a sense of violation. The intense biographical imperative of the retrospective format seemed to flout at every turn my experience of Haring from the journals. As a spectator traveling through the stages of Haring's life, I was asked to follow a life of pleasure, fear, rage, and productivity that culminated with an emblem of pleasure indistinguishable from death. The blackness of the narrow exit contrasted dramatically with the bright open space that had preceded it, the devil sperm thereby privileged as a last line gesture in the diary of Haring's life—truly the end of the line. Anger and frustration overwhelmed me when confronted with this violent end. How could this story of Haring's life feel so fundamentally at odds with my understanding of the artist? Wasn't Haring's image of the devil sperm part of his larger critique of the tyranny of Christian morality? Placed at the end of his life, was this painting not reproducing that morality even as it heroicized him? How could an exhibit that celebrated an artist who fought systemic violence against people with HIV deploy the specter of AIDS in such an irresponsible way? Perhaps I had gotten Haring's story wrong. Wasn't this exhibit the true story of his life, with all the supporting evidence of his archive? This book was very much born of these questions and my urgent need to respond to the retrospective.

Almost six years later, in 2003, the Public Theater premiered *Radiant Baby*, a musical based on Haring's biography. While this show reproduced many of the thematic elements of the Whitney retrospective, the formulaic structures and expressive sentimentality of musical theater revealed something that was only implicit in the museum show: an emphasis on the literal child as the salvific telos of Haring's life story. The musical uses Haring's *Rolling Stone* interview of 1989, in which he first publicly announced his HIV status, as its central plot device.[25] In the first act opener, Haring is nowhere to be found. An assistant fields phone calls from the magazines while a multiethnic trio of children hovers eerily about the stage, speaking as a chorus and assuming the role of Haring's art students. "We are the kids he tries to teach / We are the ones he hopes his art will be able to reach," they announce. Haring emerges onstage, pauses at the exterior to his studio, and begins a slow ballad. "How can you go forward when your heart is going back? / How can you paint color, when your future is painted black?" he sings woefully, before regaining his composure and rushing into his studio to take on his duties as artist and teacher to the expectant children. The musical unfolds from the knowledge of his HIV-positive status; this unannounced fact hovers behind every utterance, until the end of the musical, when the truth is climactically spoken to Haring's assistant and Tseng Kwong Chi. The show positions the audience as knowledgeable spectators to an inevitable outcome. Haring's HIV status, whether he chooses to admit it, is the open secret that gives life to the retelling of events and shapes the moral trajectory of the show.

The musical, for all its innocent, child-obsessed song and dance, does not shy away from sex. Haring is drawn into memories of New York as a city full of boys; in one scene, set at the legendary dance club the Paradise Garage, Carlos, a DJ who serves as the show's emblematic ethnic love interest, pushes the beat to a level that propels Haring's body into motion. Eventually Haring's life spirals out of control due to sexual excess, constant drug consumption, and a publicity machine that generates bad spin almost as quickly and voraciously as it makes him an "it boy" of the 1980s art world. "Draw me a way to see the end!" Haring pleads during a frenzied breakdown. Salvation appears in the shape of a fan letter from a twelve-year-old boy, who appears on stage to sing his appreciation. Haring realizes he must produce as much as possible in what little time he has left. Images of works from the last two years of his life flash across the stage in rapid succession. Amid a chorus dressed in white, Haring sings a closing hopeful tune before taking one final dramatic breath of air as the stage goes black.

Radiant Baby pointedly dramatizes a moral, causally coherent tale that was implicit in the Whitney retrospective. It crystallizes the ways in which Haring's desire is violated by traditional mappings of life history, oriented in what I call heteroheroic fashion toward the telos of innocent children. The heterosexual pathos of time, a concept I visit later through Roland Barthes's writing, is perfectly represented in *Radiant Baby*'s musical question of how to draw Haring's end. His HIV diagnosis heightens the stakes of his artistic production, as Haring feels slighted by the art world and harps on his lack of proper recognition among the great modern masters. His cry for esteem and attention is answered by a more meaningful calling: that of the children. This access to temporal extension through the inspiration of youth offers a convenient substitution for the literal reproduction of children while also retroactively moralizing Haring's past actions. The musical suggests that Haring's newfound life in the face of death demands he accept accountability for his sins—not in this case the generic excesses of youth but a whole era of New York City sex, fame, and celebrity. The musical's celebration of life is hardly liberated from the very attitudes that promoted and continue to promote violence against those living with HIV.[26]

These experiences with productions of Haring's life have made vivid to me the stakes of a biologically inflected imagination of biography. These narratives might not explicitly communicate the biological science behind HIV and its effects on Haring's body, but they maintain a tacit connection between the social world, Haring's activities, and the scientific consequences of HIV infection. In April 1987, Ronald Reagan resisted calls for value-neutral AIDS education with the following statement: "After all, when it comes to preventing AIDS, don't medicine and morality teach the same lessons?"[27] While the danger and implicit phobia of this statement might be obvious, the connection between morality and science has become so naturalized that one is often left with more insidious articulations of this ideology when encountering the history of those lost to AIDS. This is in part due to the teleological way a life gets defined through a causally ordered chain of events. These stagings of Haring's life literalize an idea of Keith Haring's "body of work," creating an indexical relationship between his physical body and the art he produced. They document Haring's fight against phobic understandings of HIV even as they use a narrative form that encases his life in a moral structure. In the traditional mode of the heroic male artist's biography, Haring reaches greatness through his singular ability to overcome adversity. And in Haring's case, an investment in children becomes a way to maintain a sense of legacy despite his aberrant sexual behavior and his lack of biological progeny.

In countering this narrative, I have been drawn to the archive as a vibrant resource for ordering time otherwise. My training in performance studies has deeply informed the methodological approach of this book, even as the specifically queer dimension of this project has led me to question some of the most theoretically sophisticated reflections on the performative force of the archive. In Diana Taylor's 2003 essay "'You Are Here': The DNA of Performance," for example, the performance studies theorist searches for a realm of performance work that is not wed to the discursive. Her essay argues powerfully that the idea of "the archive"—a trope that clearly partakes of the West's valorization of writing—needs to be supplemented with the idea of "the repertoire," a more embodied way of conceptualizing the historical transmission of performative effects. As Taylor's titular reference to DNA suggests, the repertoire is tied for her not only to the body but to the biological, an emphasis that suits the performance sites that interest her—among them the Madres de la Plaza de Mayo, whose well-known protests during and after Argentina's Dirty War rely on the symbolically potent reproductive connection linking the protesting bodies to the those of the disappeared.[28]

Keith Haring's Line, by contrast, remains drawn to the archive—precisely because of its textuality, and because of the queer effects that textuality sponsors. Like Taylor, I am invested in the way textual arrangement cannot fully grasp the affective dimension to the reproductions of history—desire's surplus to its textual representation. But I am wary—as many of the subjects of this book are wary—of a too-hasty reliance on the biologized body as the emblem of the performative. For those of us working with histories shaped by HIV and AIDS, the ideas of transmission and of the biological body have informed particularly charged discourses.[29] Meanwhile, the trope of lineage and futurity are deeply challenged by the queer legacies animated by Haring's archive.[30] The queer intellectuals who constitute a key part of the background to this book are obsessed with writing, and with articulating the performative potential of the future through writing. This very much includes Haring himself, who found inspiration in the experimental, performative writing practices of figures like Jean Genet, Brion Gysin, and William Burroughs.

The legacy that links these thinkers and artists to one another, and to Haring, can be conceptualized in erotic and bodily terms, but it evades any notion of a literal, procreative, or biological transmission. These are instead lines of desire and artistic possibility, and they reach into the discursive space of the archive as well. A queer desire has animated my apprenticeship in the archive, one that produces resistant vectors to universal truths embedded in historical narrative while creating associations of political possibility. There are no conclusive ends to these departures; rather, each opens a potential universe and refigures the futurity of artistic production by those who have been subsumed in moralizing narratives of remembrance. *Keith Haring's Line* is written against the impulse of traditional historical investigation, against the notion that time moves each figure and their production toward singular deaths.

A Performance Studies Scholar in the Archive

Calling attention to how art and archival imagery animate me as a scholar, I want to demonstrate what a performance studies approach to art might look like. In chapter 1, I examine multiple stages for Keith Haring's performance in New York City, including the art studio, the subway platform, and the gallery. Connecting Haring's involvement in the nightlife and performance scene of downtown New York to his public display of art production on the streets and subways platforms, I take an expansive approach to performance practice; the various scenes in which Haring was active allow me to explicitly frame Haring as a performance artist. Moreover, while I am interested in Haring's impromptu creation of theaters for his artistic performance, I also underscore the performative nature of his art. I explore how the canvases and objects he paints do something in the world, thinking through the ways in which his graphic line constitutes scenes of consumption and the subjects who come in contact with it. This includes not only Haring's lovers and collaborators in life as well as his audience (which continues to grow) but also the analyst of his work. Keith Haring's line is a mobile sign inspired by semiotic theory and cross-racial desire, and it must be understood according to its animating capacities, which continue to make themselves felt whenever the work is witnessed.

Chapter 4, "Drips, Rust, and Residue: Forms of Longing," attends to the continued performative power of Haring's line as it manifests itself in a series of objects and artworks that have been revisited or remade following his death. This final chapter pushes my methodology to its furthest limit, exploring the vital and ambivalent energy with which I continue to experience the presence of a powerful artist. In the last stretch of this introduction, I want to begin to explore the possibilities of this way of reading by returning to Warhol's Polaroids—and to my own apprehension of them—to elaborate a mode of analysis that strives to capture the continued life of Haring's line, as it at once incites a history of cross-racial desire and refuses its containment within the coherent narratives that have come to represent the life and work of the artist.

In one particular silkscreen, Warhol used multiple images from his photo session with Haring and Dubose.[31] The result is a canvas in which their bodies blur in the center, as if the two men are pulling into each other and creating another being (figure I.4). The overlapping figures formally evoke Haring's fantasy about his relationship with Dubose. If Haring understood sexual intimacy as a powerful way to become nonwhite—to inhabit the otherness of his object of desire—this artistic expression rep-

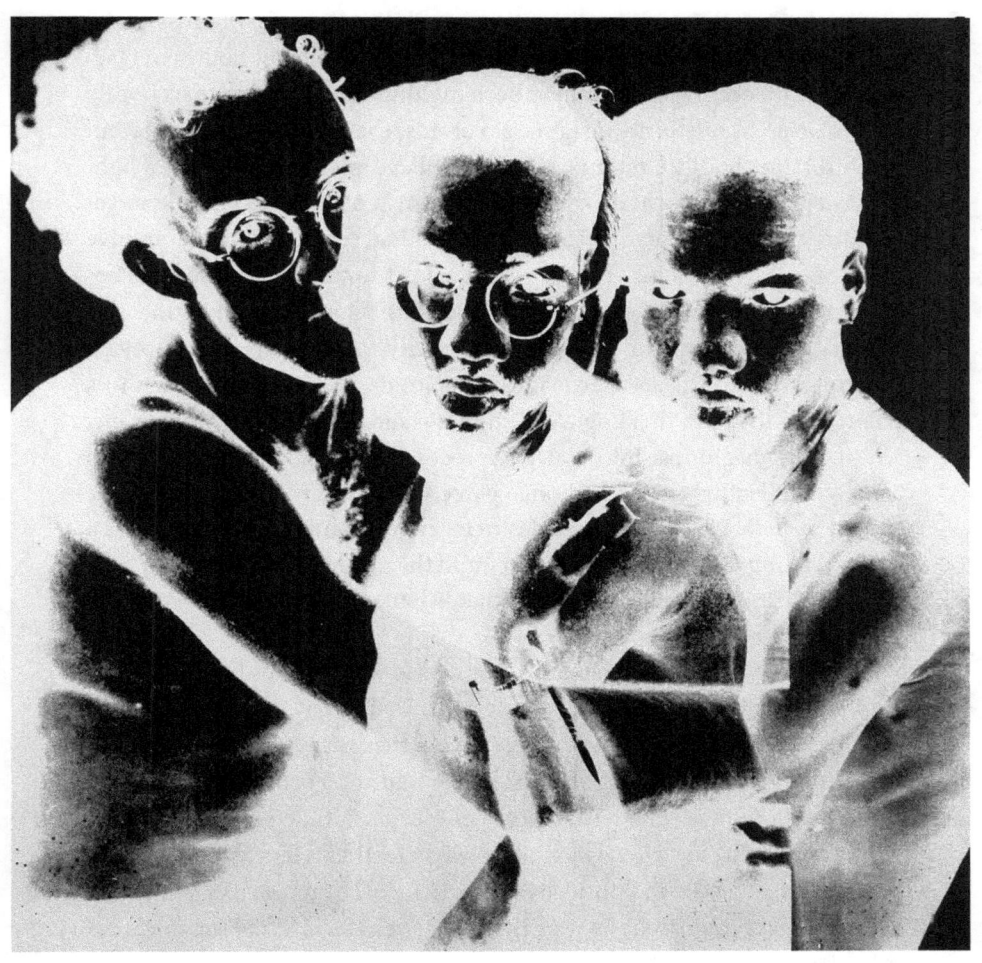

Figure I.4. Andy Warhol, *Keith Haring and Juan Dubose*, 1983. Acrylic and silkscreen ink on canvas, 40 × 40 inches. © 1983. The Andy Warhol Foundation for the Visual Arts, Inc. / Licensed by Artists Rights Society (ARS), New York.

resents a visual manifestation of that possibility. A figure of cross-racial contact seems to emerge from the distinct but convergent bodies of Haring and Dubose. Warhol's canvas both highlights and breaks apart bodily boundaries. While in the original Polaroids, the embracing lovers retain their distinct bodily contours, Warhol's collage and manipulation of light rewrites those bodies as an overlay, producing an alternate vision that yet retains the visible contours of their individual forms. Warhol's archive thus offers a trace of his creative practice. I get some sense of the steps between the capture of the image and the final silkscreen, a canvas that has always seemed to me to represent so perfectly the tensions of my project. Compared with the smaller original Polaroids, the silkscreen—with its central bodily blur, this impossible figure—suddenly seems bigger to me. Moreover, my glimpse into Warhol's process makes the silkscreen feel less coolly intellectual than I had once perceived it. I have characterized the image as indicative of Haring's desire for nonwhiteness; I believe that is a valid reading. But now I must understand the image in relation to my own desire, for it is definitely my desire that is hailed by the archival material related to Haring's life.

The animating potential of Warhol's work was perhaps best described in Roland Barthes's 1980 essay on pop art. Defined by its reproducibility and repetition, the Warholian subject in Barthes's account accesses a temporality distinct from that of classical portraiture. For Barthes, Warhol's reproductions resist the teleological conventions of historical being. The urgency of being as defined by death—what Barthes refers to as the pathos of time—is replaced in pop art by the facticity of the image itself, in which it is no longer important for a work to "be given the internal organization of a destiny (birth, life, death)." But the subject is not eradicated by this evasion of biography and teleology: "However much pop art has depersonalized the world, platitudinized objects, dehumanized images, replaced traditional craftsmanship of the canvas by machinery, some 'subject' remains. . . . The one who looks in the absence of the one who makes."[32] Naming the onlooker, the one who interprets and projects meaning onto the canvas, as the subject of the work, Barthes argues that the essence of the Warholian image is the rhetorical process through which the social world codifies the figure. Neither the artist nor his subject is essential to the art piece; rather, the work of art is its reception.

In Warhol's archive, I am left looking in the absence of those who made. Overcome with the desire to imagine, to know in some way that moment of intimacy between Haring and Dubose, I am confronted with the impossibility of knowing it, and with my own process of projection. To some degree I can name my compulsion to enter the scene of the photographs as conditioned by histories of loss and queer desire, the ongoing systemic violence against those with HIV, and the racist legacies of colonialism. Warhol's archive presents a process of mechanical reproduction around historical images and, as such, destabilizes the indexical relationship between the archival image and its referent. Like his silkscreen canvas, the documentary image from his archive demands that I engage in the act of its interpretation and interpolates me as the subject of the image. This is a scene of complicity, a complex field of negotiations in which I must accept the unknowable and pursue an interpretive project according to my desire, shaped as it is by the social worlds and histories I inhabit.

Haring, inspired by Warhol, allowed his line to be reproduced, to travel across surfaces and into the hands of consumers in the form of T-shirts, buttons, and posters. This was a utopic project where he imagined a world in which everyone could own a piece of his art. In this distribution, the line loosens itself from the artist and the moments in which he painted or drew his designs, allowing it a signifying life beyond the corporeal life of Haring himself. This continued and unpredictable life of meaning was always inherent to Haring's line, both as performance art project and as a graphic sign that indexed histories of contact and appropriation. The following story written in Haring's absence represents my attempt to articulate an understanding of the artist's life and his line, mapping fields of cross-racial desire to enliven the line beyond the limiting conditions of a singular story about the artist.

In a diary entry dated March 18, 1980, Haring discusses his obsession with the pretty boys he sees throughout the city:

> These fucking beautiful boys drive me crazy. The guy in the subway with his legs wide open in front of him—on purpose. Glancing at me and just enjoying being looked at. This guy in the cafeteria. Gorgeous. I just stand there and say "gorgeous" to myself over and over again. I find a reason to use the phone so I can stand there near him a little longer—pretty—pretty—pretty boys. And I just look and I know it's just as bad because I only look and I have an incredible imagination. I can have these boys, any of them, all of them, tonight alone in my little room in the dark—just my imagination—dark

eyes, dark hair, and gorgeous bodies, penetrating gaze. To quote an essay by Jean Genet I read recently, "Eager thick penis, rising from a bed of black curls." So writing it out. Writing it out of myself—stop thinking about it and take this energy into another form. This energy, sexual energy, may be the single strongest impulse I feel—more than art?(!)[1]

Haring paints a self-portrait here of a hormonal twenty-one-year-old art student encountering boys and the work of Genet. A maddening, churning sexual desire pulses through this vision of an agonized state of arousal. The male objects of desire frustrate him in their demands for his libidinal attentions, fueling energy in tension with the affective space of art. From the subway car to the cafeteria at the School of Visual Arts, boys are everywhere in New York City. Using a pay phone as an excuse to remain close to one of these boys, Haring demonstrates a drive toward proximity, keeping himself and the object of desire in a physical and visual relational field. His obsessive repetition of "gorgeous" and his frenzied fantasy of possessing "any of them, all of them" within the realm of his imagination communicate a manic state of arousal. This is a densely affecting scene of excitement, longing, vulnerability, frustration, and empowerment.

Referring to Genet at the end of this horny passage, Haring cites material from his intellectual pursuits as a young queer artist developing his practice; perhaps the Genet essay was required reading for one of his classes. The "eager thick penis, rising from a bed of black curls" is preceded by descriptive words—"dark hair, dark eyes, and gorgeous bodies"—that indicate something about the boys Haring possesses in his imagination. They are defined aesthetically by darkness, and in his citation of Genet, it is a bed of black curls from which an eager member rises. Bodies with dark features fill Haring's erotic imaginary, both in his apprehension and in his lonely bedroom conjuring of them. Unable to act beyond looking, Haring anticipates, seems to long for, the private moment in which he will have them, a multiplicity of dark eyes that in his possession will penetrate him. And then, after citing Genet, Haring diverts from this plan and imagines writing as the act that will evacuate the forceful urge, freeing his mind.

In some versions of the Genet essay cited by Haring, two meditations are set side by side in parallel columns. One tells the story of Genet's encounter with a man in a third-class train compartment, while the other considers Rembrandt's later paintings. Haring emulates the former, attempting to reproduce the dramatic pathos of Genet's writing. The French writer describes a quick moment in which his eyes were met accidentally by that of a filthy man who looked up briefly from his newspaper. Overcome by a terrifying feeling of disintegration in this fleeting but potently penetrating glance, Genet records that he recognized "a sort of universal identity with all men." He seems to dissolve into the traveler—"a body and face without grace, ugly, in some details even vile"—and the traveler into him.[2] A deep sadness washes over Genet as the notion of a contained self defined against that of another is corrupted, and in turn, eroticism itself seems forever destroyed. He is disgusted by the recognition of himself in all others and frightened by the loss of an eroticism that has been so central to his identity. Rembrandt's paintings, in which Genet has sensed a base animality essential to all humans, inform his understanding of what happens to him in the face of the traveler. Toward the end of his meditation, Genet confesses that the act of writing about his shocking recognition that all men are of the same value is an attempt to "rid [himself] of eroticism, to try to dislodge it." He then closes the essay with a word portrait that unfolds through a successive description of body parts, starting with the engorged penis cited by Haring, "and after that: thick thighs, then the torso, the whole body, the hands, the thumbs, then the neck, the lips, the teeth, the nose, the hair, finally the eyes that summon amorous furies as if for a rescue or an annihilation, and all that struggling against this so fragile look capable perhaps of destroying this All-Power?"[3] It is as if Genet's eyes are traveling across the surface of one of Rembrandt's paintings. This final form, emerging on the page in a manner similar to that of an artist's sketch, is ambiguously defined. It could be a representation of Genet himself, or perhaps he is redrawing the traveler, eroticizing him through a lascivious attachment to body parts and connecting this universal man to the many who have consumed him sexually. Through his writing, he poetically casts an unfixed form suspended between significations, that of the universal versus that of the erotic.

Transposing Genet's initial scene of encounter to a New York City subway car, Haring recasts himself in the role of the agonized artist whose entire being seems defined by sexual energy. Where Genet focuses on a classed dirtiness he finds vile, Haring preoccupies himself with dark-featured men who feed his libido. If qualifying features of otherness are what both enable Genet's sexual desire and shock him to the terrifying reality that he is all other men, then Haring's lustful fixation on the gorgeous bodies of New York City might too bring with it the power to realize the universal interchangeability of all men. For isn't this the story of sex and becoming he fantasizes in his intimacy with Juan Dubose? The whiteness of his skin as counter to a soul that aligns itself more closely to that of people of color reflects a tension in the racial color line—a defining border that can be overcome through a shared interiority. Haring's difference from Dubose, and potentially all those with whom he experiences a deep sexual intimacy, dissolves in the space of erotic connection. Yet, like Genet's unsettling discovery, Haring's framework for becoming the other depends on the signifiers of difference for its realization.

This chapter explores the libidinal field of Haring's art production within New York City, considering the ways in which writing and Haring's expression of line are connected to his cross-racial desire. Directly citing writing as means to evacuate his body of desire, Haring reproduces Genet's question about the power of the universal—as embodied in art—to undo the erotic. What does it mean for Haring to write it—sexual energy—out? Is the writing in the diary passage a literal act of putting pen to paper, describing scenes of encounter to free himself from the grip of all those lustful looks? Or perhaps what is described here is a kind of sublimation of desire into a different kind of writing, like that of the graffiti tag or the neoprimitive line (figure 1.1). Is this writing what occurs when chalk or brush hits a surface onto which Haring inscribes a graphic line? In this chapter, I argue that Haring's signifying line continually animates the central drama of Genet's text and Haring's citation of it. It emerges in relation to spaces of contact, zones of transport, and a legacy of queer performative writing experiments—all of which are informed by a desire for an other—while simultaneously signaling a universally transcendent form of human communication.

Analyzing the ways in which race and desire animate each other for Haring in the urban spaces of sexual contact also means looking at the writings of some of the men who came into virtual or real, sexual or verbal, contact with him. Accordingly, in this chapter, I examine the writing of performance artist and poet John Giorno (who, many years after a sexual encounter with Haring, wrote an essay about it), Samuel Delany (whose writing about gay bathhouses offers a way of thinking about energies of integration and disintegration that Haring experienced in public sex), and Roland Barthes (whose book on desire and longing offered Haring a model for "writing out" his own feelings of rejection and desire). For all of these men, experiences of desire are also experiences of race, even if in the writing out of desire each performs, the racial content of that desire

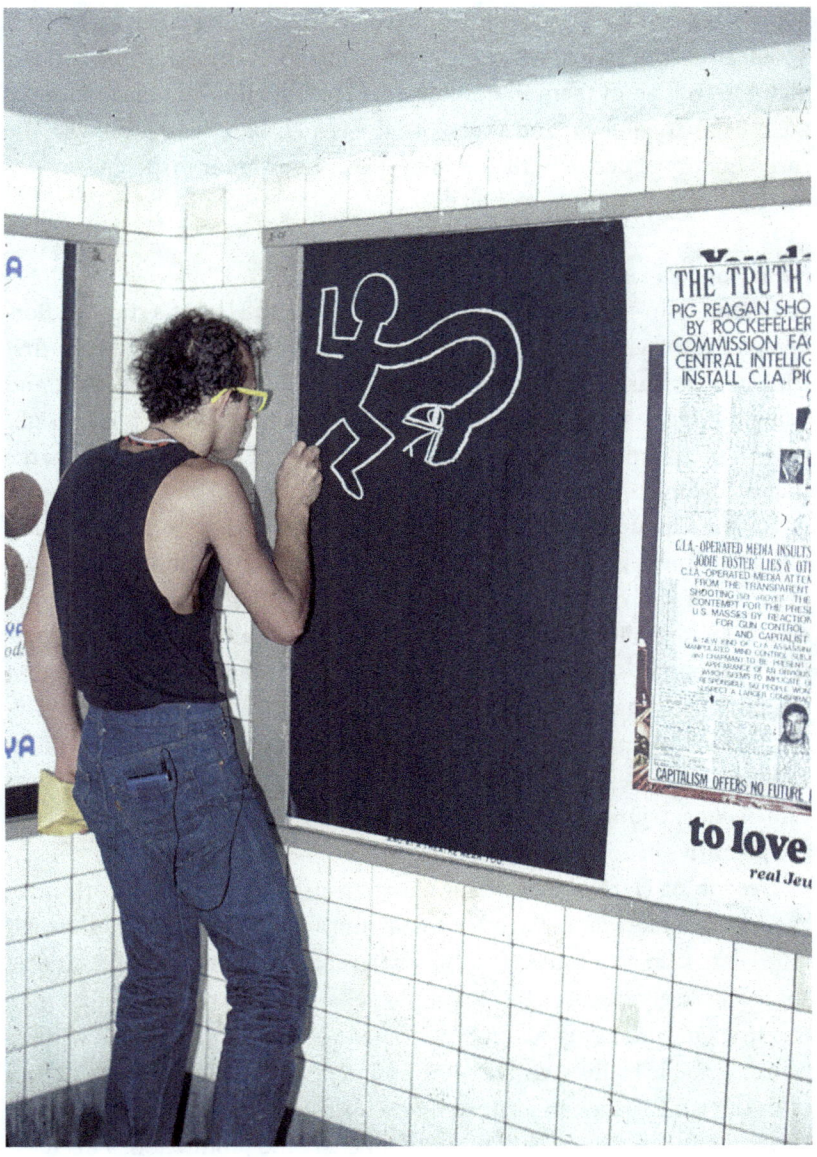

Figure 1.1. Keith Haring drawing in New York City subway, 1981. Photo by
Tseng Kwong Chi © Muna Tseng Dance Projects, Inc., www.tsengkwongchi.com.
Art by Keith Haring © The Keith Haring Foundation.

is variously occluded or acknowledged (Giorno's writing is less than frank about how race structures both his relation to Haring and his writing about it). But all of them illuminate how Haring's line—at once semiotic and visual, theoretical and experiential—is a visible negotiation with the raced quality of desire in the moving spaces of urban transport.

Keith Haring's Line

In Brion Gysin's preface to a 1985 catalog for Keith Haring's show in Bordeaux, the experimental writer and calligraphic artist describes the first time he saw Haring produce a line on a wall. The two were in Paris, and using a Magic Marker, Haring drew his signature tag, "his copyright Baby," in "the midst of a wild tangle of the local French graffiti," marks that according to Gysin were "in emulation of New York." Gysin is in awe of Haring's mode of inscription, surprised by what the live act of tagging reveals. "Lines can be drawn or pulled or written or scribbled or, nowadays, be sprayed out of a can," he writes. "Keith Haring's line is something else. It looks a bit like an engraved line or a sculpted line but it is not either of them. It is a carved line, like the one the man made when he first used it to cut what he wanted out of the air in the back of the cave."[4] Gysin, describing Haring's line as carved and likening the cave wall bison to Haring's trademark radiant baby, suggests a depth that exceeds two dimensions, trying to make sense of the line through a comparison with the primitive act of cave drawing.

Describing Haring's line, many observers use some idea of the primitive as a way to make sense of it, often imparting a mythical weight to Haring's gift. He is seen as a sorcerer in his virtuosic capacity to size up available space and freely execute a line in proportionate scale to whatever surface he touches. One need only see archival footage of Haring in action to witness his remarkable facility with the line and to understand the kinetic appeal of the artist. Engaged in a stunning exercise of improvisational drawing, Haring fascinated audiences through an energetic production. This mesmerizing force imbued his art, those traces of his physical performance, with an animating quality that spoke to something profoundly human for those who came in contact with it. The ineffable aspect of the work, which Gysin indicates through a comparison with the cave man's inscription, appears to resist logical explanation. This invocation of the primitive (an invocation that many subsequent critics have repeated) reduces the work's communicative abilities to the nonintellectual and precivilized.

These attributions of "primitiveness," of the basically "human," to Haring's line are a fantasy, even as they respond to the undeniable charisma of Haring's performance. Such reductions indicate that his line is already imbued with discourse; it is not a transcendental, universal manifestation of Haring's timeless connection to the spirit of man but instead a citational line that communicates this idea through its historical travels. Haring devoted himself to the performance of citation and honed his drawing skills according to a studied understanding of sign systems. The art historian who recognizes this labels Haring's work "neoprimitive," calling attention to the various indigenous and prehistorical artifacts that share a visual affinity with his art. For example, Maarten van de Guchte demonstrates how the tribal arts of Central and South America, including pottery and painted cloth, bear a resemblance to Haring's works.[5] Van de Guchte constructs a convincing visual argument for the artist's appropriation of preexisting, non-Western expressive visual culture. He turns to James Clifford's critique of MOMA's 1984 *Primitivism* exhibition, in which Clifford claims that the West's display of primitive artifacts is a modernist technology through which the non-Western is produced as such. Van de Guchte understands Haring's citation of tribal art from across the globe as a challenge to the institutionalized mode of Western appropriation described by Clifford.[6] Haring recycles primitive sign systems and deterritorializes the line, demonstrating "a sensitivity for picking up signals" and creating work that moves between the gallery, the club, and the streets.

Haring's art does in fact disperse primitive inscriptions, potentially disrupting the line's indexical relationship to the tribal and premodern. That said, the recognition of this does not negate the line's capacity to reinscribe a fantasy of the non-Western other onto the surfaces Haring paints. Also, Haring's appeal beyond established art world environments, part of his enduring legacy as a globally accessible popular artist, often reinforces a vision of Haring as someone connected to a universal and primitive mode of communication. Within this framework, Haring produces sign systems that are seen as utterly human in their ability to communicate to even the most "uncivilized" viewers. Moreover, his line reveals the ways in which a non-Western visual imaginary is inextricable from the West's own recognition of itself. In other words, Haring's citational line embodies the condition of the Western self that can only be recognized through a dialectical relationship with a premodern tribal other. This other is both at the limits of Western man's consciousness and that which the westerner has constructed as the purely human.

The signifying drama of Haring's neoprimitive line is the production of the nonethnic self within and against a fantasy of tribal inscriptions' ties to noncivilized cultures. In the terms of Michael Omi and Howard Winant's theory of racialization, Haring's line could be understood as an ambivalent racial project.[7] It represents a signifying system of otherness that is inherently connected to historical movements and that reproduces an ongoing social demarcation of difference within relational fields of power. Insofar as tribal inscriptions and artifacts indicate the cultural production of nonwhite subjects, Haring's carved line invokes a space of racialization, codified as it is by a larger history of appropriation and display.[8] Haring recognizes his whiteness as that which is counter to his spirit and soul. In many ways, the line enacts this story of Western selfhood, one that is hardly unique to Haring's erotic inclination for people of color. His art indexes and participates in a historical visual system of racialization where the primitive line signifies nonwhite uncivilized expression. It also represents that which is somehow inherently interior to whiteness, revealing what is obscured in the Western subject's civilized condition. It is both what Haring fundamentally is and that which he is not. In his particular articulation and expression of writing, Haring's line makes explicit what is inherent to every discourse of the primitive, a foundational Western self that is necessarily constructed through an erotic field of cross-racial appropriation.

In a 1986 journal entry, Haring connects the idea of the primitive to a "social responsibility" he finds "in the LINE itself." Stating that he hates the word "primitive" to describe a culture, he argues that his wide acceptance as a public figure depends on the line's communicative capacity in a world technologically distanced from "so-called 'primitive' cultures."[9] Informed by a 1951 lecture that Jean Dubuffet gave at the Arts Club of Chicago, in which the French primitivist uses the art of the "savage" to criticize a Western history of aesthetics, Haring believes that his art has the potential to illuminate "a common denominator that runs through all time, all peoples."[10] What Haring describes as the social responsibility of the line is its critical humanist capacity. In its evocation of the primitive, he believes that his line connects its audiences to the universal spirit of art, making visible the ways in which the construction and justification of different cultures and different religions distance people from a true experience of the world. Chapter 2, on Haring's relationship with graffiti artist LA II, focuses on the explicitly racialized discourse produced around the line of graffiti within this larger rhetoric of humanist expression. Here, in keeping with Haring's citation of Genet, I examine another kind of appropriated line, that of the queer figures who inspired Haring's writing projects and his erotic imagination of the city.

Poetic Experimentation and Zones of Transport

In a singular exhibition on Haring's first four years in New York City (1978–82), Raphaela Platow organized a show, first exhibited in 2010 in Vienna, that showcased Haring's development of a graphic vocabulary of recombinant figures. The journal entries and works on display demonstrated Haring's studied play with visual codes. Within the focused time frame covered by the show, Haring created an alphabet of line drawings that were repeated and reorganized to different effects, and Platow expertly situated this work in relation to the larger world of creative influence that Haring claims in his journals. In her catalog essay, the curator maps a trajectory between Haring's initial experimentation with visual signs and a text-driven performance art practice that would come to shape his career as an artist known for transforming the cityscape, tying his use of Brion Gysin's and William Burroughs's cut-up method poetry in his distribution of photocopied image-text across the streets of lower Manhattan, for example, to his semiotic-theory-inspired production of recurring figures like the radiant baby and barking dog on subway platforms. "The switch from abstract shapes," Platow writes, "facilitated Haring's return full circle to figures and objects, now conceived as linguistic elements that could engage with one another in a multitude of ways."[11]

A look at the pages of Haring's journals throughout the focal period of Platow's exhibit reveals a dizzying number of references to writers, artist friends, and educators who shaped and fed Haring's creative practice. Recovering from hepatitis in his hometown of Kutztown, Pennsylvania, on September 1, 1979, Haring meditates on his previous year in New York City and contemplates all that he has experienced as an emerging artist. "I have been enlightened, I have fallen into poetry and it has swallowed me up," he writes before describing what he refers to as "THE CHUNK CALLED POETRY"[12] (figures 1.2–1.7). Rather than produce a concise definition, Haring creates a free-associative list of experiences, texts, concepts, and names, which is electrifying and exhausting in its scope and evocation of the particular ethos of downtown New York City at the time. Below is a fraction of material cited from the pages-long entry:

It started with JOHN GIORNO and BURROUGHS at the Nova Convention in December 1978, It's reading CAGE and starting my first four cassettes at SVA in February. It's the poetries of video-tape and BARBARA BUCKNER. It's BURROUGHS and GINSBERG and GIORNO upstairs at the MUDD CLUB. . . . It's ART SIN BOY and CLUB 57 POETRY READINGS EVERY WEDNESDAY NIGHT THIS SUMMER. It's reading SAINT GENET by SARTRE on the subway going to work in QUEENS. . . . It's BOOKS THAT YOU JUST FIND IN a LIBRARY . . . BOOKS THAT FIND YOU. . . . It's HAVING DINNER ON AVENUE C WITH DINA, DOZO, AND FUGACHAN (a MAN). It's thinking about SEX as ART and ART as SEX. It's continued situations and controlled environments, B-52s, BATHS, AND SEX WITH FRIENDS. . . . It's understanding painting. IT'S SOMEONE YELLING "LICK FAT BOYS." . . . It's seeing TRISHA BROWN DANCE. IT'S ITALIAN FILMS FROM 1967. IT'S LAURIE ANDERSON AT MUDD CLUB. It's NEW MUSIC, NEW WORK at the KITCHEN for a week. . . . IT'S XEROXES PUT UP IN the West Village for Gay Pride weekend and hearing people that had seen them months later. . . . IT'S GRAFFITI IN THE SUBWAY. It's riding the BUS FROM KUTZTOWN TO N.Y.C. . . . IT'S ANONYMOUS SEX. . . . It's a new understanding. IT'S BEGINNING A SEED A GARDEN IT'S THE BIG CHUNK CALLED POETRY.

In this journal entry, venues such as the Mudd Club and Club 57, where Haring did spoken-word performance and organized art shows, appear next to the names of galleries and the artists who showed in them. From Patti Smith to the B-52s to John Giorno to Laurie Anderson to Matisse, Haring maps his influences within a network of geographies and inspirational acts that include public sex, bathhouses, having "sex with friends," "taping up Xeroxes walking home drunk," and "letting records skip for ten minutes . . . thinking it's beautiful." Poetry here is not limited to exercises in textual arrangement but rather a more expansive vision of what might be enacted or performed in the world through the performative capacities of signs and how one codifies personal experience in language. Haring collages text and experience with what feels like an open call for the reader to take up his references and to explore this open field of poetry. What this passage indicates and what Platow's exhibit makes palpable is how poetry for Haring becomes inseparable from his inspired painting practice. In fact, the painted line is a vehicle for poetry. His figures are displayed as an open gestural sign system that he imagines as inherently incomplete and in need of an audience of individuals who will produce endless configurations of meaning in their apprehension of them.

To get a sharper sense of how Haring's poetic and painterly line opens itself to the pulsions of otherness, I want to turn briefly to another moment of writing out of desire—John Giorno's account of subway sex with Haring. Superficially similar to Haring's written records of urban sex and desire, Giorno's writing also shows how such writing can work to close down or limit its openness to the difference—especially racial difference—that underwrites it. In his 1994 collection of poetry and prose, *You Got to Burn to Shine*, Giorno details an encounter with Keith Haring in the Prince Street subway station men's room. Entitled "Great Anonymous Sex," the piece begins with Giorno's remembrance of a dinner he hosted in January 1985 in honor of William Burroughs. While the event, which involved several famous gay men, was an awkward disaster for Giorno, he remembers enjoying Haring's enthusiasm. Introducing the piece, Giorno cannot resist discussing the fact that Haring arrived with Juan Dubose and that both had been up all the previous night at the Paradise Garage. According to Giorno, Dubose was crashing—coming down from a high—and spent most of the evening on the stairs in the hallway "sleeping with his head in his hands."[13] The following day Giorno and James Grauerholz visit Haring's studio at 611 Broadway. Haring, wishing to thank Giorno for the impact he has had on his life, presents him with a painting of a "man with a big dick at the end of which was a hand holding a baby."[14] Giorno is quite taken with this gift and begins to meditate on why Haring seems so familiar to him, the previous night having been the most sustained contact with him that he remembers. Then, it occurs to Giorno that they had "had intense sex, almost a love affair, for over an hour, a long time for subway sex on the run."[15]

What follows is a thick description from memory of Giorno's encounter with Haring on a morning in July 1982, when Giorno decided to make one of his common stops in the men's toilet at the Prince Street station. The prose conjures a steamy encounter, where a young Haring remains intent on Giorno's pleasure as men all around them engage in sexual activity. The summer heat is intensified in the humid underground toilet that "stank of cigarette smoke, disinfectant, and piss."[16] Giorno's continual re-

---

Figures 1.2–1.7. Haring journal, "THE CHUNK CALLED POETRY," September 1, 1979. Writing by Keith Haring © The Keith Haring Foundation. **On the following pages.**

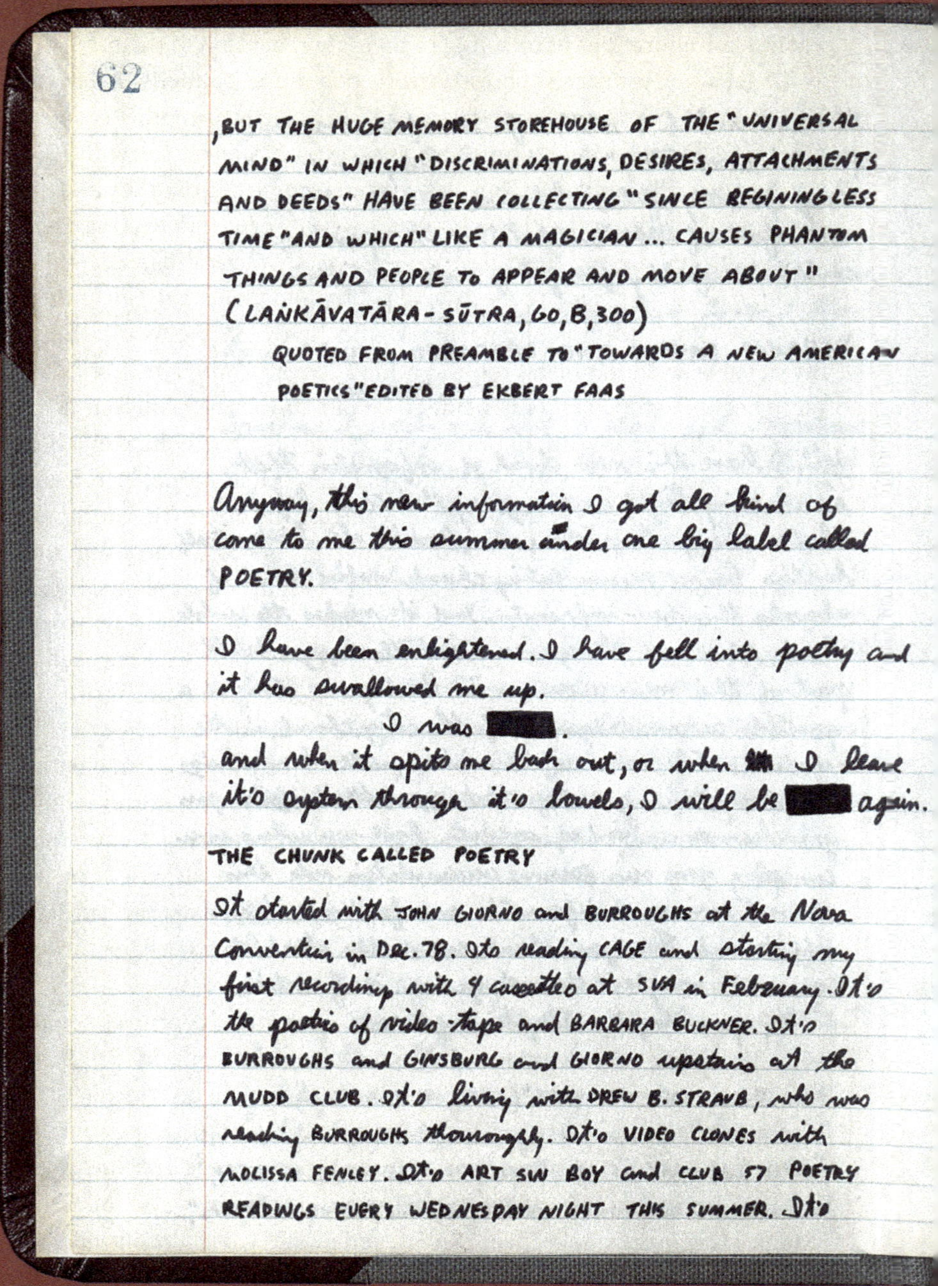

62

,BUT THE HUGE MEMORY STOREHOUSE OF THE "UNIVERSAL
MIND" IN WHICH "DISCRIMINATIONS, DESIRES, ATTACHMENTS
AND DEEDS" HAVE BEEN COLLECTING "SINCE BEGININGLESS
TIME "AND WHICH" LIKE A MAGICIAN ... CAUSES PHANTOM
THINGS AND PEOPLE TO APPEAR AND MOVE ABOUT "
(LAṄKĀVATĀRA - SŪTRA, 60, B, 300)
    QUOTED FROM PREAMBLE TO "TOWARDS A NEW AMERICAN
    POETICS"EDITED BY EKBERT FAAS

Anyway, this new information I got all kind of
come to me this summer under one big label called
POETRY.

I have been enlightened. I have fell into poetry and
it has swallowed me up.
         I was ▮▮▮.
and when it spits me back out, or when I leave
it's system through it's bowels, I will be ▮▮▮ again.

THE CHUNK CALLED POETRY

It started with JOHN GIORNO and BURROUGHS at the Nova
Convention in DEC. 78. It's reading CAGE and starting my
first recording with 4 cassettes at SVA in February. It's
the poetics of video-tape and BARBARA BUCKNER. It's
BURROUGHS and GINSBURG and GIORNO upstairs at the
MUDD CLUB. It's living with DREW B. STRAUB, who was
reading BURROUGHS thouroughly. It's VIDEO CLONES with
MOLISSA FENLEY. It's ART SW BOY and CLUB 57 POETRY
READINGS EVERY WEDNESDAY NIGHT THIS SUMMER. It's

Figure 1.2

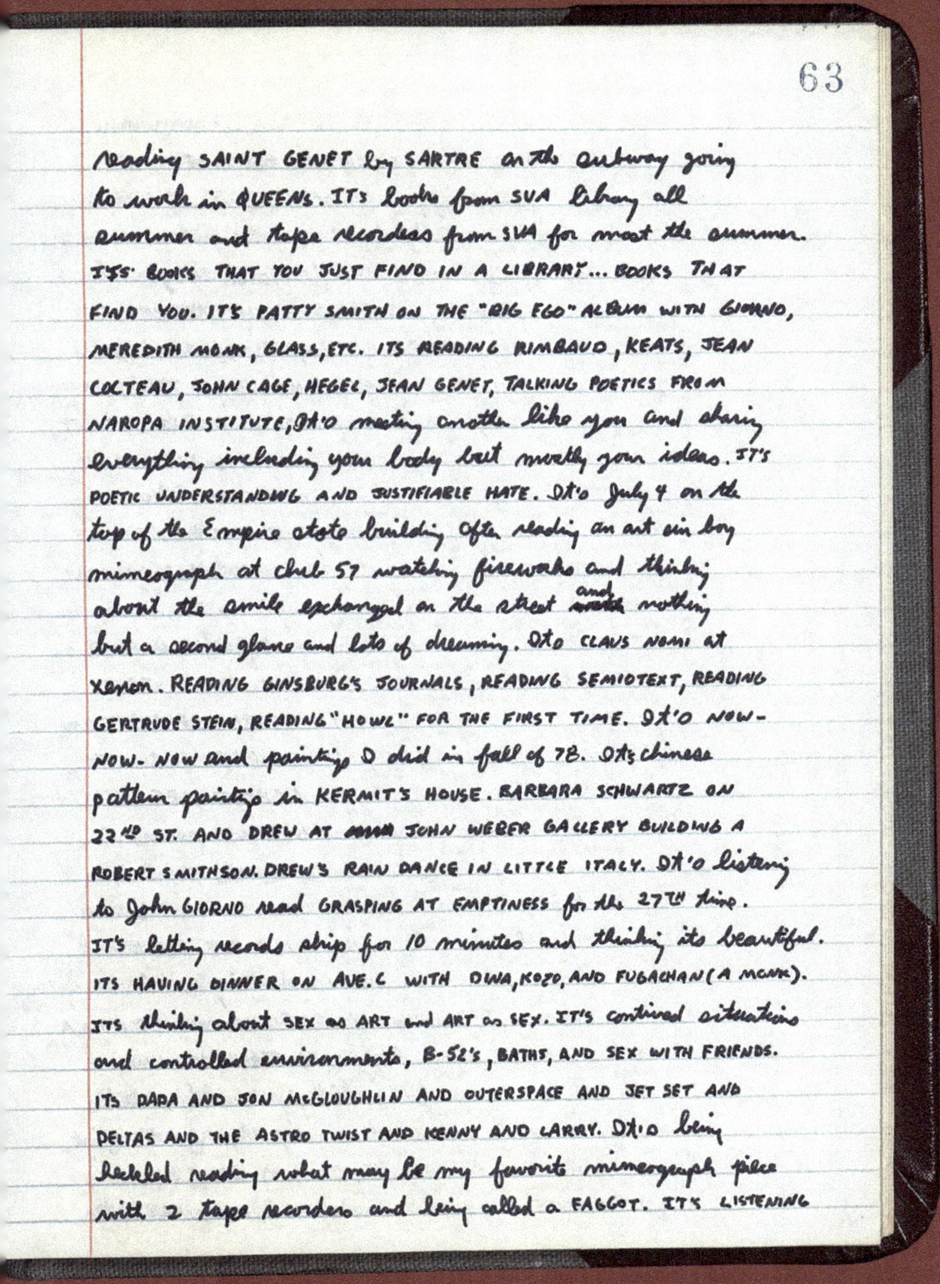

reading SAINT GENET by SARTRE on the subway going to work in QUEENS. ITs books from SVA library all summer and tape recorders from SVA for most the summer. IT'S BOOKS THAT YOU JUST FIND IN A LIBRARY... BOOKS THAT FIND YOU. IT'S PATTY SMITH ON THE "BIG EGO" ALBUM WITH GIORNO, MEREDITH MONK, GLASS, ETC. ITS READING RIMBAUD, KEATS, JEAN COCTEAU, JOHN CAGE, HEGEL, JEAN GENET, TALKING POETICS FROM NAROPA INSTITUTE, It's meeting another like you and sharing everything including your body but mostly your ideas. IT'S POETIC UNDERSTANDING AND JUSTIFIABLE HATE. It's July 4 on the top of the Empire state building after reading an art zine boy mimeograph at club 57 watching fireworks and thinking about the smile exchanged on the street and with nothing but a second glance and lots of dreaming. It's CLAUS NOMI at XENON. READING GINSBURG'S JOURNALS, READING SEMIOTEXT, READING GERTRUDE STEIN, READING "HOWL" FOR THE FIRST TIME. It's NOW-NOW. NOW and painting I did in fall of 78. It's chinese pattern painting in KERMIT'S HOUSE. BARBARA SCHWARTZ ON 22nd ST. AND DREW AT JOHN WEBER GALLERY BUILDING A ROBERT SMITHSON. DREW'S RAIN DANCE IN LITTLE ITALY. It's listening to John GIORNO read GRASPING AT EMPTINESS for the 27th time. IT'S letting records skip for 10 minutes and thinking its beautiful. ITS HAVING DINNER ON AVE. C WITH DWA, KOZO, AND FUGACHAN (A MONK). ITS thinking about SEX as ART and ART as SEX. IT'S contrived situations and controlled environments, B-52's, BATHS, AND SEX WITH FRIENDS. ITs DADA AND JON McGLOUGHLIN AND OUTERSPACE AND JET SET AND DELTAS AND THE ASTRO TWIST AND KENNY AND LARRY. It's being heckled reading what may be my favorite mimeograph piece with 2 tape recorders and being called a FAGGOT. ITS LISTENING

Figure 1.3

TO OTHER POETS AT CLUB 57. TALKING TO POETS. BEING A POET AT CLUB 57. ITS painting on ST. MARK'S aside of STROMBOLI PIZZA. It's having one night at CLUB 57 when everyone in the open reading was in top form and everyone knows and everyone is smiling. ITS HAL SIEROWITZ READING. IT'S BEING QOTED IN HIS POEM AS SAYING, "I CONSIDER MYSELF MORE OF AN ARTIST THAN A POET, SAID KEITH". IT'S MAKING XEROXS and mimeographs. ITS MEETING CHARLES STANLEY AND BEING APPREHENSIVE. IT'S TAPING UP XEROXS WALKING HOME DRUNK. It's looking in the window at BUDDHA. It'D seeing A TRUCK THAT SAYS "BETTER METHODS". IT'S BUYING JEROME ROTHENBERG'S BOOK "TECHNICIANS OF THE SACRED" that BARBARA BUCHNER had lent to me in spring and now TIM MILLER has it out of the library and now I'm reading reference to it in a new book I bought. ITS ALL THOSE THINGS THAT FIT TOGETHER SO PERFECTLY THAT IT APPEARS PRE-DETERMINE ITS DREAMS OF FALLING INTO WARM WATER HOLE WITH EXOTIC FISH CREATURE AND ENOUGH LIGHT TO SEE EVERYTHIN It's finding HANDBILLS ABOUT SIN that are poems in themselves. It's painting on walls in the suburbs. IT'S The bridge in LONG ISLAND CITY WITH 1958 AND 1980 on parallel poles. IT'S FINDING OUT THE SPACE AGE BEGAN IN 1958. It's STEVE PAXTON dancing in the sculpture garden at MOMA. IT'S CARL ANDRE POEMS IN THE MOMA SUMMER SCULPTURE SHOW. It's JONES BEACH ON SUNDAYS. ITS MATISSE. ITS MATISSE. It's listening to old cassettes I made in winter and understanding them for the first time. A NOTION OF PROPHECY. ITS DOUGLAS DAVIS' ARTICLE IN THE VILLAGE VOICE about post-modern art. "POST-ART." It's A

pornographic pictures and black feathers. It's GERMANY.
It's JAPAN. It's hearing DOW JONES AND THE INDUSTRIALS. It's
loose joints and conversations. IT'S THE SAME THING, THE SAME
THING. It's understanding painting. ITS SOMEONE YELLING
"LICK FAT BOYS". ITS CONVERSATIONS ABOUT ALL ART BEING PRETENTIOUS.
It's not going to look at ART in the galleries all summer. IT'S seeing
drawings by KEVIN CRAWFORD AND DREW B. STRAUB and
thinking about the relationship. ITS THINKING ABOUT THE RELATIONSHIP
BETWEEN SEEMINGLY UNRELATED OBJECTS AND EVENTS. It's an
art "context". It's thinking about poetry on as many different
levels as I can. It's thinking about myself. It's comparisons
and ratios and mathematical principles. ITS THE POETRY OF
NUMBERS. Language, culture, time, spirit, universe. ITS THE
PAST PRESENT FUTURE ALL TIME NO TIME SAME THING. It's
systems within systems that evoke systems. ORDER - FORM -
STRUCTURE - MATTER. It's seeing TRISHIA BROWN DANCE. ITS
ITALIAN FILMS FROM 1967. It's LAURIA ANDERSON AT MUDD CLUB. It's
NEW MUSIC, NEW YORK at the KITCHEN for a week. IT'S CHARLIE
MORROWS PIECE FOR 60 CLARINETS AT BATTERY PARK IN CELEBRATION
OF THE FIRST DAY OF SUMMER AT SUNSET. It's the BRONX ZOO.
Reading RIMBAUDS LETTERS. Reading RIMBAUDS ILLUMINATIONS ON
THE SUBWAY AND IN A CAFE EATIN' CREAMORATA AND DRINKING
PERRIER. ITS FELLINI FILMS WITH QUAN CHI. It's finding things
on the street. ITS CONVERSATION WITH LYN UMLAUF ABOUT THE
NOW NOW NOW TAPES AT J. WEBER GALLERY SHOW. ITS XEROXS PUT
UP in the west village for gay pride weekend and hearing people
that had seen them months later. ITS THE NINTH CIRCLE AFTER
THE GAY PRIDE MARCH TALKING ABOUT APATHY AND MILITANCY. It's
wearing and distributing red & white stripes for one evening.
ITS READING AT CLUB 57 WHILE THIS WOMAN who I later found

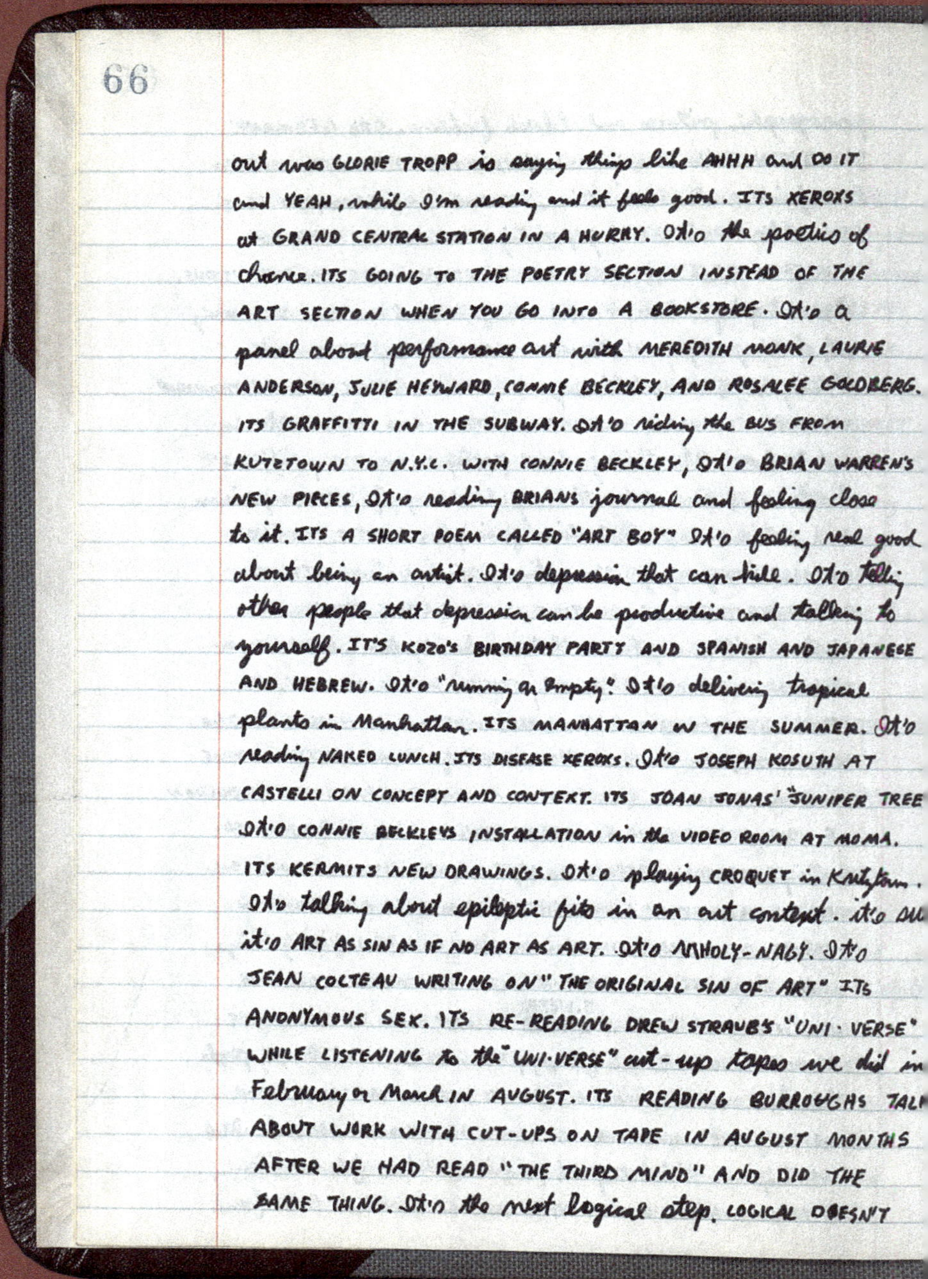

out was GLORIE TROPP is saying things like AHHH and DO IT
and YEAH, while I'm reading and it feels good. ITS XEROXS
at GRAND CENTRAL STATION IN A HURRY. It's the poetics of
chance. ITS GOING TO THE POETRY SECTION INSTEAD OF THE
ART SECTION WHEN YOU GO INTO A BOOKSTORE. It's a
panel about performance art with MEREDITH MONK, LAURIE
ANDERSON, JULIE HEYWARD, CONNIE BECKLEY, AND ROSALEE GOLDBERG.
ITS GRAFFITTI IN THE SUBWAY. It's riding the bus from
KUTZTOWN TO N.Y.C. WITH CONNIE BECKLEY, It's BRIAN WARREN'S
NEW PIECES, It's reading BRIANS journal and feeling close
to it. ITS A SHORT POEM CALLED "ART BOY" It's feeling real good
about being an artist. It's depression that can kill. It's telling
other people that depression can be productive and talking to
yourself. IT'S KOZO'S BIRTHDAY PARTY AND SPANISH AND JAPANESE
AND HEBREW. It's "running on empty". It's delivering tropical
plants in Manhattan. ITS MANHATTAN IN THE SUMMER. It's
reading NAKED LUNCH. ITS DISEASE XEROXS. It's JOSEPH KOSUTH AT
CASTELLI ON CONCEPT AND CONTEXT. ITS JOAN JONAS' JUNIPER TREE
It's CONNIE BECKLEYS INSTALLATION in the VIDEO ROOM AT MOMA.
ITS KERMITS NEW DRAWINGS. It's playing CROQUET in Kutztown.
It's talking about epileptic fits in an art context. it's all
it's ART AS SIN AS IF NO ART AS ART. It's MOHOLY-NAGY. It's
JEAN COCTEAU WRITING ON "THE ORIGINAL SIN OF ART" ITS
ANONYMOUS SEX. ITS RE-READING DREW STRAUB'S "UNI-VERSE"
WHILE LISTENING to the "UNI-VERSE" cut-up tapes we did in
February or March IN AUGUST. ITS READING BURROUGHS TALK
ABOUT WORK WITH CUT-UPS ON TAPE IN AUGUST MONTHS
AFTER WE HAD READ "THE THIRD MIND" AND DID THE
SAME THING. It's the next logical step. LOGICAL DOESN'T

Figure 1.6

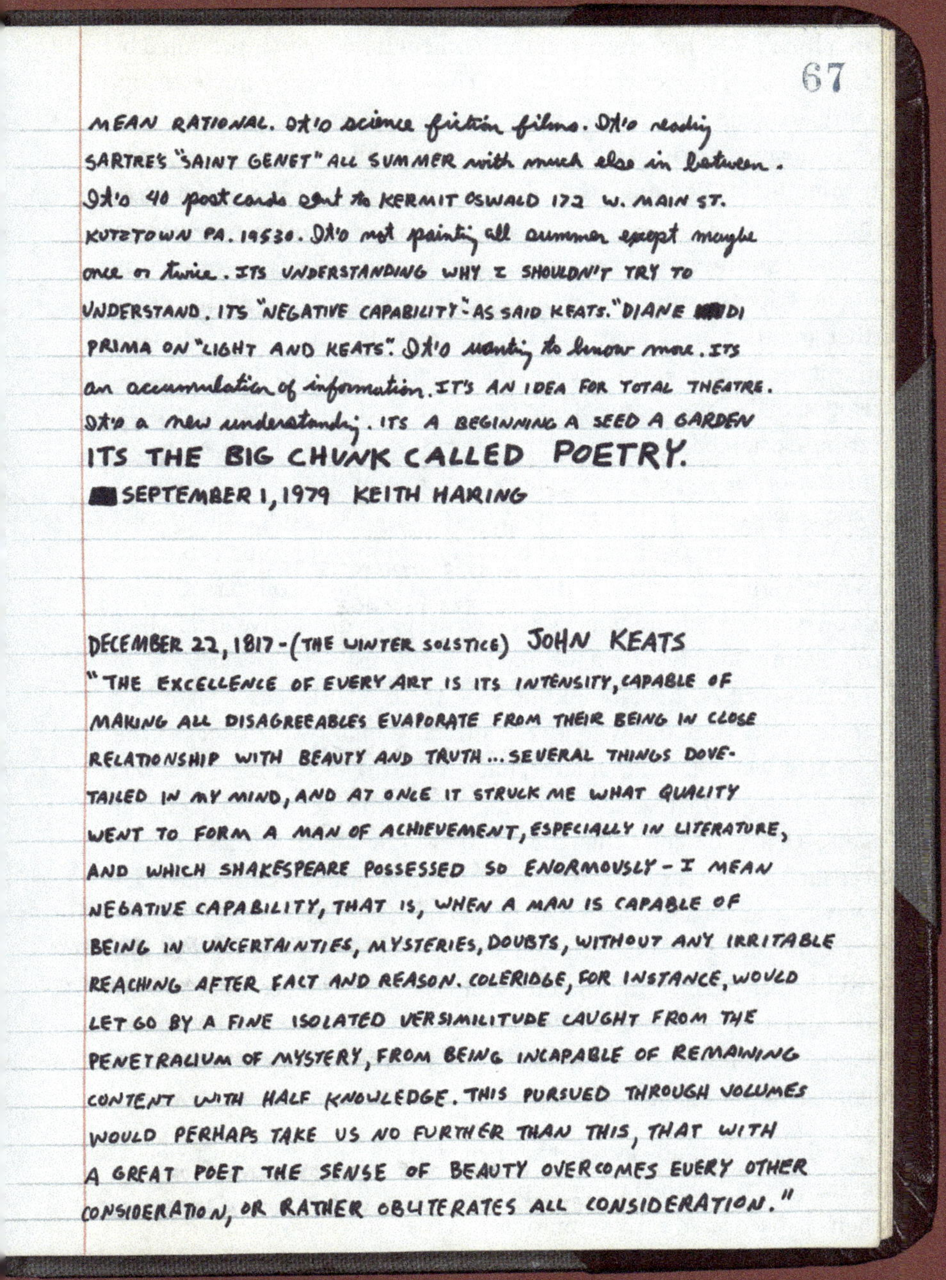

MEAN RATIONAL. It's science fiction films. It's reading
SARTRE'S "SAINT GENET" ALL SUMMER with much else in between.
It's 40 postcards sent to KERMIT OSWALD 172 W. MAIN ST.
KUTZTOWN PA. 19530. It's not painting all summer except maybe
once or twice. ITS UNDERSTANDING WHY I SHOULDN'T TRY TO
UNDERSTAND. ITS "NEGATIVE CAPABILITY" AS SAID KEATS. "DIANE DI
PRIMA ON "LIGHT AND KEATS". It's wanting to know more. ITS
an accumulation of information. IT'S AN IDEA FOR TOTAL THEATRE.
It's a new understanding. ITS A BEGINNING A SEED A GARDEN

ITS THE BIG CHUNK CALLED POETRY.
■ SEPTEMBER 1, 1979 KEITH HARING

DECEMBER 22, 1817 - (THE WINTER SOLSTICE) JOHN KEATS
"THE EXCELLENCE OF EVERY ART IS ITS INTENSITY, CAPABLE OF
MAKING ALL DISAGREEABLES EVAPORATE FROM THEIR BEING IN CLOSE
RELATIONSHIP WITH BEAUTY AND TRUTH... SEVERAL THINGS DOVE-
TAILED IN MY MIND, AND AT ONCE IT STRUCK ME WHAT QUALITY
WENT TO FORM A MAN OF ACHIEVEMENT, ESPECIALLY IN LITERATURE,
AND WHICH SHAKESPEARE POSSESSED SO ENORMOUSLY - I MEAN
NEGATIVE CAPABILITY, THAT IS, WHEN A MAN IS CAPABLE OF
BEING IN UNCERTAINTIES, MYSTERIES, DOUBTS, WITHOUT ANY IRRITABLE
REACHING AFTER FACT AND REASON. COLERIDGE, FOR INSTANCE, WOULD
LET GO BY A FINE ISOLATED VERSIMILITUDE CAUGHT FROM THE
PENETRALIUM OF MYSTERY, FROM BEING INCAPABLE OF REMAINING
CONTENT WITH HALF KNOWLEDGE. THIS PURSUED THROUGH VOLUMES
WOULD PERHAPS TAKE US NO FURTHER THAN THIS, THAT WITH
A GREAT POET THE SENSE OF BEAUTY OVERCOMES EVERY OTHER
CONSIDERATION, OR RATHER OBLITERATES ALL CONSIDERATION."

Figure 1.7

turn to the quality of heat in the bathroom scene conveys a fevered build toward climax. The importance of the moment for Giorno is indicated by the appearance of the collection's title: "The kid and I were completely hyperventilated, and our body temperatures burned, and we poured sweat, which is always an exhilarating high. You got to burn to shine. We got to burn some more. Burning away all concepts, releasing bliss trapped in our hearts."[17]

Giorno evocatively plays with the choreography of public sex, taking time to describe the specific movements of bodies in space, how they come together and then break apart as a new person enters and they wait to determine if the newcomer is a threat to their illegal activity. In the alternating description of the larger scene of homoerotic contact and the specific details of Haring's sustained attention to him, Giorno emerges as a kind of director and master of the scene of debauchery. Make no mistake: this is Giorno's fantastic recollection. In this memory, Haring is an idolizing, enthusiastic lover whose clear recognition of Giorno compromises to some extent the anonymity Giorno cherishes in the public men's room encounters. Giorno insists on painting Haring as awkward and harps on distinctive details that portray a humbling portrait of the now famous artist. "His eyeglasses were getting crunched on his face and he took them off. He was a plain boy with pale, white skin, but with a very attractive quality. . . . I sucked the kid's cock (it was cut, not that large, but very hard)."[18] And later: "He was wearing a white T-shirt, washed-out blue jeans with holes at the knees, and sneakers. An art student, I thought again, as I saw some splashes of paint on his pant leg." The sex intensifies, and Giorno eventually slides into Haring's Vaseline-lubed ass. After ejaculating, Giorno is less than enthusiastic about reciprocating the intensity and attention Haring displays. "The kid pressed his dick against me, and obviously wanted to come, too. I sucked his cock and wish he'd come so I could stop doing it."[19] Eventually, Haring does cum, and Giorno swallows the "thick gooey" delivery. Giorno then meditates on AIDS and presumes contact with HIV during their encounter:

> The Prince Street subway toilet happened in 1982 and we know from the record that Keith Haring suspected he was HIV positive in 1981, when he discovered early symptoms of AIDS, such as swollen lymph glands and thrush. When I gave Keith the blow job, he was HIV positive. Keith died of AIDS on February 16, 1990. Even though I swallowed his cum, somehow now in 1993 I am HIV negative and in excellent health, one of many miracles.[20]

This particular paragraph jars me in its strange reliance on a discourse of objectivity. Using what "we know from the record," Giorno insists on his contact with HIV via Haring, and then describes a miraculous re-emergence from the underground toilet without contraction of the virus. Giorno fashions himself officially into Haring's lifeline, citing the exact date of his death and speculating on the date of Haring's suspected HIV infection. Many would argue that Giorno's story promotes an HIV-phobic misrepresentation of risk; the lack of Giorno's seroconversion is hardly a miracle, given the acts described here, even if Haring had been HIV positive.

The recollection of subway sex constantly shifts between grand ideas of union and transcendence through sex and what comes off as a somewhat patronizing portrait of Haring. Giorno's tone represents a catty gay way of relating to fame, which is to say, Giorno wants to ride the proximity to Haring and his fame but only by asserting control over the situation he describes and placing Haring in a subservient position. Further, Giorno inserts himself quite grandly into Haring's life through an insistence on being of historical importance for having swallowed a celebrity viral load and lived to tell the tale. Giorno is certainly part of the line of legacy for Haring, explicitly in his connection to William Burroughs, Brion Gysin, and Andy Warhol—key figures who deeply shaped Haring's understanding of underground creativity and resistant aesthetic practice.[21] Yet, much of his meditation here on what he shared with Haring is clearly projection and fantasy. The tone of his story in many ways echoes the "john" subjectivity I detail when discussing Samuel Delany and trade later in this book.[22]

While I am critical of the retelling, resisting the prose as a testament to what really occurred, Giorno's intense and poetic recollection is a model intervention in how Haring's life and sexuality are bound to official narrative. In many ways, my writing about Haring also plays in a tricky space of assertion, in which I detail how Haring's sexual activity and desire are always connected to race. My story here cannot be verified according to the record, but rather I write about a fantasy I too share. Giorno's narrative constructs a representation that embodies many of the recurring myths that surround Haring as an iconic figure. For instance, Haring's innocent enthusiasm, be it sexual or artistic, appears as one of the most seductive traits for those who were in contact with him. In Giorno's remembrance, he harnesses this trait as a way to convey the realm of transcendence that occurred in their sexual exchange, when he writes, for example, "I have always remembered that anonymous kid for opening himself so extraordinarily, for allowing a great moment of fabulous transcendent sex, motivated by genuine love, trying to radiate enough compassion to fill the world."[23]

In many ways Giorno's record of sex with Haring fits in the tradition of urban writing that Marshall Berman famously identified with Baudelaire in his well-known analysis of the modern city, *All That Is Solid Melts into Air*. In his chapter on the Haussmannization of Paris, Berman discusses how poor neighborhoods were demolished as the new boulevards cut across the city, exposing the wealthy and the disadvantaged to each other in novel ways. The greater cross-traffic of differently classed bodies facilitated anonymity even as it increased a network of gazes. Berman reads Baudelaire's "Loss of a Halo" as a descriptive poem that captures the affective geographies in formation for the poet in this period of urbanization. The prose poem concerns a poet and a man who happen to recognize each other in "*un mauvais lieu*, a disreputable or sinister place, probably a brothel."[24] The poet describes having lost his halo in the "mire of the macadam" while dodging the bustling traffic of the city. Having lost this signifier of greatness, he is free to enter into the dark places of ordinary men, such as the one he confronts now. Berman sees this encounter as one that evokes the possibility increased traffic and contact afford the modern poet, who eagerly distances himself from the idea that great art represents a communion with the spiritual greatness of all that is holy. The poet leaves his halo behind to explore the fecund underworld of commoners and chastises those artists who fail to lose their halos in the maelstrom of traffic.

"Great Anonymous Sex" echoes Baudelaire's "Loss of a Halo" in the sense that the artist's spiritual relation with the world emerges from an active engagement with the lowliest of people and places. In Berman's reading of Baudelaire, he argues that the modern city forces movement on everyone and "enforces new modes of freedom."[25] Baudelaire shows how the man willing to engage fully in new opportunities for movement and connection will experience a great expansion of opportunity. The subway toilet in which Giorno, the well-regarded poet, encounters the lowly art student represents *un mauvais lieu*. Maneuvering subway train flows and the traffic of bodies in transit, the contemporary modern poet ducks into a rank toilet to discover the pure bliss of anonymous connection. Here, he is recognized as a serious literary figure by someone he does not know and allows himself to be taken into the movement that surrounds him, finding

the transcendent and miraculous in the very details of base bodily exploration. The spiritual and material converge in the meditation on sexual
life, exchange of fluids, and the choreography of bodies in space.

In Baudelaire's prose poem, and Berman's analysis of it, class is the
central boundary of difference that the modern city puts into agitated
movement. For Haring, race was an equally central concern. This fact is
reflected—if only obliquely—in Giorno's narrative. Immediately following the discussion of subway sex, Giorno remarks on an encounter he had
with a black man at the Everard Baths. The meeting with Haring and the
one with this nameless black man are tied for Giorno to all the other "great
countless sexual encounters." Giorno's notions of transcendence and the
liberating possibilities of sexual encounter happen between black and
white. Here lies a defining trio: Haring, the black man, and Giorno acting
as "the combat troops of love liberating the world."[26] While Giorno wished
to have sex with Haring again, he claims he never mentioned it, particularly because he knew of Haring's "obsession" with black and Latino boys.
Here, at the end of the prose piece, Giorno quotes part of the passage I
cited in the introduction: "I firmly believe that a sexual relationship—a
deep sexual relationship—is a way of truly experiencing another person—
and really *becoming* that other person." "And I agree with him," writes
Giorno as the closing statement for this affecting account.[27]

The quotation from Haring appears both strangely embedded within
a racial discussion and distant from it. Giorno seems to suggest a kind of
becoming that happened between the two of them and perhaps the countless becomings that are symbolized by Haring and the black man. In Gru-
en's biography of Haring, the quotation Giorno cites here is directly tied
to Juan Dubose; it is Haring's intimacy with Dubose that occasions this
discussion of sexual activity as mode of becoming. But Dubose is oddly
occluded by Giorno in the panegyric to toilet sex that climaxes with this
quotation. As we have seen, Giorno takes the time to delineate a space of
gay sociality from which Dubose is excluded: while Haring charms the
dinner host with his enthusiasm, Dubose crashes in the hallway, suffering
a fall from whatever high was experienced the night before at the Paradise Garage. Dubose has been written into the periphery at the opening of
"Great Anonymous Sex" and, at the end, is displaced yet again as Giorno
associates his sexual memory with Haring's ideas of becoming without
the explicit reference to Dubose. In an important sense, race has intervened at every key moment of his relation to Haring—both preventing
that relation's continuance and providing the verbal terms that Giorno

would eventually use to memorialize it: Haring's proclivity for brown boys is a deterrent to further advances by Giorno and a condition of possibility for the intensity with which Giorno can describe their encounter at the Prince Street toilet. As the man unfamiliar with Haring or his sexual tastes, Giorno indulges Haring's earnest enthusiasm in sex. What then has each of these figures become in Giorno's projection of the past? Has Giorno more fully become Haring, knowing him perhaps better than simple details of his life could ever offer? In fact, it is the break from anonymity, the knowledge of Haring's life, that prevents this more primal knowledge of being. This is what Giorno is playing with here in the discussion of anonymity. Details of a life, of a history of cross-racial contact and contraction of disease, intervene in the choreography of sex and potential for future becoming. Giorno's deployment and disregard of Dubose echo many of the ways in which Dubose exists as a defining and necessary figure in the romantic view of Haring as transcendent interracial lover, while being ignored and somewhat disposable in the setting of valued exchange between those in an esteemed gay artistic circle.

Boys in the Baths: Lines of Desire in the Radiant City

As we have seen, Haring's poetic practice is shaped by his sexual encounters in the city. His artistic output is deeply informed by his contact with men in spaces of sexual subculture, and his development as an artist unfolds in relation to an emotional negotiation with mundane and exceptional circuits of intimacy. Not only does Haring physically alter the New York City landscape through his poetic practices broadly understood, he also uses its locations and the experiences they enable as material for his writing experiments. This is nowhere more visible than in his writing about the St. Mark's Baths, the famous East Village venue that Haring frequented and that has been central to many queer figures' recollections of a mythic downtown sex life. Like the Paradise Garage dance club, the St. Mark's Baths has become a historical landmark in a queer imagination of the potential for sexual collectivities; its impact continues to reverberate long after it was closed down by the New York City Health Department in 1985 because of fears surrounding HIV transmission. In this final section, I turn to other writers who have thought through the political potential of public sex and further explore Haring's practice of writing out desire, specifically through a journal passage about an encounter at the St. Mark's Baths.

The St. Mark's Baths, as it appears in Samuel Delany's memoir, *The Motion of Light in Water*, has provided performance scholars such as José Esteban Muñoz and Fred Moten an opportunity to think about the radical potential of queer sex, specifically in terms of an aesthetic mapping of the future as it relates to Allan Kaprow's performance piece "18 Happenings in 6 Parts," which Delany first saw in the late summer of 1960.[28] Delany recalls the performance from what he admits is a hazy memory. Within the performance room, six chambers had been created for audiences to occupy. The polyethylene walls that divided audience members from one another effectively prevented Delany from seeing fully what occurred in the other chambers, but sound, light, and movement could be registered through these temporary walls. Later, in 1963, Delany is reminded of this experience when he visits the St. Mark's Baths, with its dark rooms filled with writhing bodies and its partitioned architecture. Men could be sensed and felt in different rooms, but the actual number of bodies in the space could only be imagined. Delany describes it as a scene of libidinal saturation, in which the mass of bodies was "not only kinesthetic but visible."[29] This, in turn, provokes another memory of sexual encounter along the West Side piers, where men would meet under the cover of dark, finding each other in the spaces between trucks that parked there overnight. In the moment of a police raid, a mass of bodies emerged from the darkness, a number far greater than the eight or nine men reportedly arrested.

Kaprow's avant-garde staging of fragmentation and the kind of fragmentation Delany witnesses in public sex spaces like the West End piers and the St. Mark's Baths evoke for Delany a larger political condition for those engaged in illicit sexual activity. In the spaces of public sex, bodies in contact remain partially visible in dark lighting but still enable one to imagine a mass of men coming together within a larger sphere of social repression. Muñoz, in his essay "The Future in the Present," picks up this thread in Delany's memoir to illuminate the ways in which contemporary political agendas for "quality of life" continue to undermine the conditions for a visible, coherent sexual counterculture. Looking to a Queens, New York, queer male strip club, the police disruption of a Matthew Shepard rally, and a stickering campaign by an activist queer collective, Muñoz articulates these sites as political critiques of the present that offer utopic potential through material and imagined queer community formation.[30] Moten's project, meanwhile, explores how Delany constructs an imagined world that counters the supposed transparency of experience. The felt but not starkly visible mass of bodies represents a politically viable, resistant mass of "perverts," whose full visibility as a collective is made impossible by the institutional structures that isolate these bodies from each other. And yet, it is the isolating structures of partial visibility that make possible the very experience of a collective to be imagined. In this "double distinction" of impossibility and possibility, Moten finds a productive framework to think about a larger tradition of improvisation in black avant-garde aesthetics.[31]

As for Delany, Haring's experiences at the St. Mark's Baths and other spaces of sexual exploration facilitate his understanding of a self in relation to the larger world he inhabits. The baths are an essential part of "THE BIG CHUNK CALLED POETRY," an environment of contact and improvisation where what is felt moves beyond the walls of this particular space of public intimacies and into Haring's writing of, in, and on the city. A key figure in Haring's writing about these issues turns out to be Roland Barthes, whose work on semiotics Haring first encountered as a student at SVA and referred to repeatedly in his journals. In another 1979 entry reproduced in the catalog for Platow's exhibit, for example, he writes, "Love: Roland Barthes: *A Lover's Discourse*, Communication: 1. to yourself, 2. a loved object, 3. other people." He notes the fragment from the book in which Barthes relates a fable about "a mandarin [who] fell in love with a courtesan." In this fable, the courtesan promises herself to the suitor on the condition that he wait in her garden for one hundred days. On the ninety-ninth day, he leaves.[32] "The time spent waiting was the love," Haring writes, before drawing a group of penises surrounded by hearts and lines. Next to these drawn emblems of love and sex, the phrase "WAITING FOR AN ANSWER" hovers in quotation marks (figure 1.8). Beneath this heading, Haring writes the following words: "and I said I'm getting bored. I'm going home. WAITING FOR A LONG TIME. WAITING. HE SAID."

The scene is a bleak one, but the visual amalgam of words and image—an amalgam apparently inspired at least in part by Haring's reading of Barthes—pulses with a strange energy. The penises and hearts huddle in a kind of hive or swarm, the space between and around them filled in with rectangular clusters of three or four short parallel lines, which seem to enclose these emblems of love and sex and pulse with those emblems' erotic and emotional energy. A key part of this page's power derives from its intermingling of semantic and visual codes. The despairing words—"WAITING FOR A LONG TIME"—are set in a startlingly exuberant visual field: the spaces between the notebook lines are filled with horizontal lines that ap-

was the love.

"WAITING FOR

AN ANSWER"

was the love.

and I said, "I'm getting bored. I'm going home."

WAITING FOR A LONG TIME. WAITING. HE SAID.

assignment:
    decode a personal mythology in terms of its meaning
        example: disco roller-skating

PERSONAL
IDEAOLOGY — an individual set
of ~~values and~~ quantitative and
qualitative values and ideas. ~~is~~

---

pear to be drawn in yellow highlighter, as if the energy of the hearts and hard-ons has come to animate the words themselves.

In this transfer of energy between word and image, line of text and visual line, Barthes's work seems key. Haring understands the scene of suspension, the period of waiting to possess the love interest, as a temporal sign that is in fact what love is. Here the sign of love coincides with desire insofar as desire is a performative condition of the not yet realized. Haring, in his processing of Barthes, sees the performance of love as a practice of visible potential in the isolated figure of the one who performs want through waiting. Waiting in this system of signs and scene of communication represents a kind of line in suspension, that which proceeds and moves toward knowing what it might mean to have one's desire realized with and through another being—but never arrives at that knowledge as an accomplished fact.

Returning to Barthes in a later journal entry, dated February 20, 1980, Haring writes his own fragment of a lover's discourse. Like the citation of Genet that opens this chapter, Haring's entry rewrites the philosophical inquiry from his studies, bringing Barthes to the baths. The following is Haring's Barthesian meditation on desire and rejection:

after the Baths in Semiotics class

Again it was the same and I feel just the same again. Waiting for an answer. And you can say all you want to. I'm not saying anything. And we sit and talk about Barthes' "Lover's Discourse." And I experienced all these signs—condensed—last night and I guess always again. And it's just the way you knew it was. Nothing has changed—it's still the same thing. But I'm tired—and feel guilty about being tired of it. But it hurts like it hurts for everyone. Distance and no more hope. O.K., give up—go home. He doesn't want you—and it wasn't just that—the right moves never happened. . . . So he gets up and leaves and I've done it too—I've been on that side before. So why are you still talking. You've been in his shoes just one more rejection but this time it's not me who is feeling powerful. . . . It has been the only thing in my head since this happened—this thing has crushed me. A misunderstanding, he said. I am nauseous with chilled stunted exaltation, I said. Sometimes I'm really happy. When? He said. I can't remember if—I'm not sure he. . . . He said soul. I said I'm going home. And how can this boy from the baths make me be in this place—and if he hadn't gotten up and walked away would you be better and didn't you cause it to happen—didn't you inflict the wound yourself? Sometimes I feel really stupid and sometimes I know I am—But you boy in the baths—you turned me inside out again and exposed myself—to myself—and I guess that's good again.[33]

The passage illuminates, once again, the emotional and intellectual potential inherent in the space of public sex. As in the passage that opens this chapter, we see Haring here in an agonized dance of self-deprecation and shame; the loved one has shunned Haring, and the unfulfilled intimacy takes on a rather dire tone in his recollection. But what is most surprising about the scene may be that it ends in suggestion of hopeful self-realization, in the startling claim that this scene is pointing to something "that's good again." Haring's creative impulses and his sustained engagement with the philosophy he encountered during his art school training at sva are elaborated through his self-exposure in rejection.

Unlike Giorno's self-possessed rendering of public sex in the Prince Street bathroom, or for that matter, Delany's description of libidinal saturation, Haring's experience at the St. Mark's Baths points to a coinciding reality—for all that bathhouses and public toilets signify for gay men, they still manage to produce feelings of isolation and rejection. Haring's account through the Barthesian fragment documents less a transcendent time of dissolving into a mass of bodies and more a drawing out of waiting, an anticipation that is often all the more painful given that pleasure and intimacy are supposedly there for the taking. If Haring expertly conjured the spirit of Genet in his own rewriting of the train, here he keenly reproduces Barthes's performance of isolation in feeling. In the juxtaposition between "He said soul" and "I said I'm going home"—a statement repeated from his previous journal entry about *A Lover's Discourse* and the fragment on waiting—Haring indicates something of a vexed relationship to the access of the interiority of the other. This is another scene of being seen in the city where Haring is worked up in his desire for another body. But the Barthesian doubt about the possibility of communion also issues in a curious potentializing of this scene of frustration. Here again we see Haring writing out his desire—even in its impossibility—and transforming it into another kind of potential. It is a directional line from a feeling of self-recrimination and doubt to a more realized sense of self, born of and immersed in the agonizing force of erotic desire but somehow not caught in it.

In his rendering of the bathhouse scene, Haring not only gestures toward a temporal space of performed affection, or lack thereof, he also engages in an act of identification—what Barthes describes in *A Lover's Discourse* as that which occurs when "the subject painfully identifies himself with some person (or character) who occupies the same position as himself in the amorous structure."[34] For Barthes, the field of identification cuts across bodies and subject positions such that the lover not only identifies with those who are in love but also with those who have been loved and failed to return affection. The lover sees himself in the one who longs for the other and the one who shuns, rejects, and causes pain. This process of identification recalls the movement Genet describes in his realization that he is like all other men, and Haring's ability to see himself as the perpetrator of rejection becomes part of laying bare the mechanisms of desire, such that erotic energy, with all its agitating force, can be transformed from the individual experience into a sense of an animated and animating structure with multiple participants.

Haring's engagements with Barthes and Genet indicate a striking capacity to think detachedly and critically about desire and his relationship to those bodies that animate fantasies of possession and becoming. What then do we make of Haring's descriptions of cross-racial contact, in which sexual intimacy with people of color allows him to become something other than white at the level of his interiority or soul? Wouldn't he recognize these ideas as affecting fantasies that arise precisely within a racialized field of sign systems? In this chapter, I have argued that Haring's line is also a performative engagement with the color line, and that that engagement is most interesting for the way it takes its definitive energy from the impossibility of the desire of merger that animates it: the color line for Haring can never really be overcome but instead acts as a signifying barrier between bodies that suspends him in difference; the seductive potential of the line's dissolution churns desire for the other, but ultimately that other can be revealed only as product of his impossible desire to have and to be something other than white.

Haring's journals repeatedly testify to the impossibility of knowing the other through desire, even as they speak to the continual rebirth of that fantasy. It is appropriate, then, that a neoprimitive line emerges as the primary vehicle for Haring's line drawing across the city. These signs in states of suspension on the subway platform perform a gestural desire; they are not (as in Giorno's recollections) a confident assertion of desire's fulfillment and desire's meaning but an incomplete expression waiting for an audience to communicate with them. Haring's line is animated by the impossibility of its coming to rest in conceptual certainty: this writing of rejection, inspired by Barthes, is full of the failure to become one with another through contact; but it is no less full of the potential for what the other offers. Haring's bathhouse fragment looks forward ("that's good") but it is fraught with doubt ("I guess") and the sense that this movement forward will also be a ceaselessly recursive process: "I guess that's good again." The individual is not dissolved into the other but sent into a space of endless difference and endless fantasy of its overcoming. Signatures from the artist's hand, Haring's markings animate a desire for something universal, namely the universal condition of difference. They cannot overcome that desire, or close it down, or declare its death or its satisfaction. Instead, they set the stage for a collective project, indicate a directionality, perform a movement: this is Haring's line.

John Gruen's authorized biography of Haring describes the artist's contact and collaboration with a young Puerto Rican graffiti artist named Angel Ortiz, also known as LA II (sometimes LA 2). Haring was seduced by LA II's signature, which he encountered throughout New York's East Village at a time when he was hanging out with notable graffiti artists like Fab Five Freddy. Amazed to find that the tagger was only fourteen years old, Haring took LA II under his wing and encouraged the young artist to collaborate with him. Between 1982 and 1984, they produced hundreds of canvases and art objects together. This is the same period in which Haring established himself as a major commodity within an international art market. As a crucial contributor to his mentor's success, LA II accompanied Haring on his global travels and produced work onsite with him.

In an interview John Gruen conducted for his Haring biography, LA II recounts the day a neighborhood friend told him that the "guy with the baby" was looking for him. LA II finds Haring working on a mural at P.S. 22 and timidly approaches. He asks Haring if he is the one looking for LA II. Haring enthusiastically responds, and LA II introduces himself. Before Haring can be convinced that this fourteen-year-old boy is the artist behind the tag, LA II must produce his line. "So I took one of his markers," LA II reports, "and wrote my signature. And *boom*! Right there, he said, 'I can't believe it's you!'"[1] In this moment, LA II is identified via his tag—what Craig Castleman in his study of New York City graffiti describes as a "writer's name in stylized letters that are gathered together in the style of a logo or monogram."[2] Ortiz's most common tags, "LAROCK" and "LA II," appear on multiple surfaces in the archive of Haring's art. Given Haring's line-driven aesthetic, it is no wonder the artist was drawn to LA II's bold expression of graffiti. The younger artist's work asserts his presence through a gestural fluidity, an animate line that signals the movement and flow of the larger hip-hop world from which it emerges. Not unlike the radiating lines that often surround Haring's human outline forms, LA II's tags seem to pulse with an animate force, appearing anything but static. After Haring meets LA II—an entity verified through his embodied gestural production—the two begin working together on projects that encode surfaces and objects with a hip-hop-inspired aesthetic. A kinetic conversation emerges across the lines of the two artists, one that conveys Haring's enthusiastic embrace of hip-hop while also displaying a dynamic and energetic exchange with LA II.

One of their most striking productions is a gold fiberglass sarcophagus onto which Haring drew crawling babies, human figures, angels, dogs, monkeys, and television sets. Laid over this Egyptian-themed form, Haring's figures take on a hieroglyphic nature. A close view of the head of the sarcophagus reveals LA II's contributions. The tags "LA ROCK" and "LAII" appear everywhere, filling in the negative space within and around Haring's outline forms. The tagger also reshaped his tag to fit in smaller areas, adding arrows that enhanced the directionality of Haring's line while incorporating bold stars into the overall design. Those who had seen Haring's subway drawings would recognize the figures he reproduced here, but LA II occupied those shapes that had become part of Haring's visual vocabulary with his own signature. In doing so, LA II added a new dimension to Haring's neoprimitive line and its signifying capacity. LA II's authentic ties, both geographic and racial, to "the street" reinforced Haring's own status as an artist intimately engaged with the hip-hop culture of New York City.

In addition to amplifying Haring's street cred, LA II entered a social world that recognized Haring's proclivity for dark-skinned boys. Haring's sexuality was a fundamental part of his public narrative, and the interviews and public statements given by LA II in subsequent years suggest that the younger artist felt the need to assert his heterosexuality against the default perception that he was one of Haring's lovers, even as he engaged in what could be described as a queer economy of exchange. The inseparability of Haring's racially motivated libidinal drives from his utopic longing for something better than the current realities of white supremacy shaped the scene of artistic complicity. Haring's identification as something other than white arises not only through networks of intimacy but also via a history of white violence against bodies of color (a topic I explore in chapter 4 in a discussion of the murder of graffiti artist Michael Stewart, which deeply angered and affected Haring). Haring's artistic partnership with LA II provided the older artist with the ultimate sidekick; theirs was not the erotic coupling of gay lovers, but their union was infused with the highly erotic, racially charged, and objectifying force of the art market's consumption and Haring's own liberal fantasies of contact. Situating LA II within the larger framework of Haring's success—one that played off the artist's relationship to graffiti and hip-hop aesthetics—in this chapter, I think through LA II's position as "trade"—a gay-slang term I take here to designate a relation of power and of exchange: a mobile, animated energy this book's introduction theorizes as complicity. My goal is to consider LA II's contributions through the lens of commodity and sexual fetishism, while also exploring the ways in which LA II engaged and continues to engage Haring's line as a means to his own success and his own artistic project.

The racial politics of graffiti have of course been central in accounts of Haring's development. The discursive field produced in popular writing about graffiti—a field structured by both fear and appreciation—implicitly attaches graffiti to black and Latinx bodies. Dagmawi Woubshet, in his recent account of Haring's work, argues that the terms on which Haring's art is appreciated often depend on a racial subtext that situates Haring as an anomaly among graffiti writers. "It was [Haring's] race that helped to give intelligence to his art and, by way of synecdoche—for he too painted in New York City's subway system—to graffiti art in general." Haring's whiteness, he argues, "extracted the threats of graffiti," tying the white art-school-trained artist to an underclass of raced others.[3]

Woubshet usefully illuminates the racialized logic of the 1980s discourse around graffiti and its mainstreaming. We can see that logic operating in an account of Haring's relation to graffiti written during the artist's lifetime: the curator and art historian Henry Geldzahler's introduction to *Art In Transit*, a 1984 collaborative project in which Tseng Kwong Chi documented Haring's subway work. Where much of the contemporary media saw subway graffiti as pure vandalism, Haring's primitive pictures emerged for Geldzahler as imagery for the people. "Radiant Babies, Barking Dogs, and Zapping Spacecraft, drawn simply and with great authority, have entered the minds and memories of thousands of New Yorkers."[4] According to Geldzahler, Haring's decision to refrain from signing his drawings reflects a communal impulse that stands in sharp contrast to the commodity signage of advertising—but also, Geldzahler asserts, to the self-advertisement of graffiti writers. Geldzahler's piece thus discusses a larger duality in Haring's work. Creating a visual vocabulary that communicates to the masses while garnering praise from more elite art circles, Haring becomes an ideal mediator between the street and the high art market. Haring's use of the line is distinct from the more commonplace tags with which New Yorkers had become familiar: for Geldzahler, the artist's creative line drawings are "driven by the hunger to communicate to a popular audience—one that lay outside the official art world."[5]

One of my claims in this chapter is that Haring's mediation between the space of the gallery and that of the street was fundamentally inflected by his sexuality and the racialized form its expression took. Indeed, immediately following this description of Haring's hunger, Geldzahler turns to the theme of sexuality, claiming that Haring's work expresses a "sexual energy [that is] so powerful a part of our natures that in the healthy world Haring projects there is nothing to hide; indeed exuberance abounds"— even as Geldzahler goes on to suggest that Haring refused to draw sexually explicit material in the subway for fear of endangering the children who like his art.[6] This chapter argues that the play between the competing binaries that Geldzahler identifies—subway versus gallery, art world versus popular culture, graffiti versus art-school-inspired signs, sexual iconography versus child-friendly imagery—communicates the very condition of Haring's production. Haring's line emerges precisely in these constitutive oppositions.

As a primary space for the enactment of graffiti, the subway was one prime setting for the production of Haring's line. Performing his art in a space discursively produced as a racialized world of threat and criminality, Haring actively engaged a theater of otherness.[7] Haring performed within and against the lines of other taggers, producing a tag that brought with it a visibility markedly different than that of the other writers in the subway. As Geldzahler's essay makes perfectly clear, this is at once a scene of contact and one of differentiation: Haring's line separates itself from the graffiti tag that is the condition of possibility for his image as a public artist. Within this field, LA II becomes complicit in a scene of art production that fetishizes his brown body and embraces the signifying capacity of his "authentically" produced line—which is to say the "real" line of "the street" with all its danger and suggestion of violation.

In this chapter, I use the concept of trade to explore that complicity precisely because it makes visible an exchange, a scene in which power differentials (of race and economic position particularly) operate but do so unstably. The communion of Haring and LA II's lines does not negate the racialized fantasy of LA II's graffiti line, even as he might appear safe within the system of appreciation that comes to value his graffiti. The simultaneously dangerous and available body of LA II fuels the cross-racial erotic energy inherent in Haring's neoprimitive line, and this suspension allows LA II to occupy a trade position in the patronizing exchange between artists. I read their collaborative work as an aesthetic manifestation of Haring's cross-racial desire and his eagerness to engage a visual vocabulary of otherness. To flesh out the fraught ethical and sexual issues implied in trade aesthetics, I look at work by the writer Samuel Delany and the photographer Philip-Lorca diCorcia; in these artists' projects, trade emerges as a scene of agential volatility, in which the structures of power that set the terms for the exchange also create the terms for the complicitous movement of power between and among the participants. The canvases Haring and LA II produced together render that space graphically visible; the interpenetrating writing they performed on the artworks' surfaces exemplifies the volatility and mobility of trade aesthetics.

A Queer Exchange

In positioning LA II as "trade" vis-à-vis Haring, I am placing the young graffiti artist within a larger history of homosocial and homoerotic contact, one structured by changing social codes that have generated what we can call an aesthetics of trade. In George Chauncey's history of gay New York, he traces the various meanings of the term "trade" from 1890 to 1940. The term refers to a multiplicity of sexual identifications and practices, including men who paid for sex with male prostitutes, straight-identified prostitutes who serviced gay men, and straight-identified men who enjoyed having sex with gay men without the exchange of money.[8] Trade, with its historically shifting meanings and connotations, indexes a sexual economy in which the nature of encounter changes; it is a capacious signifier in which multiple acts and types of sexual relations remain at play. The slippery relationship between LA II and Haring, and LA II's constant struggle to remain visible alongside a highly commodified and popular figure, can be understood in terms of this open signification.

In *Homolexis: A Historical and Cultural Lexicon of Homosexuality*, art historian Wayne Dynes provides the following entry for the term "trade":

Persons who have recently turned to homosexual behavior or who refuse to be identified as such and therefore only reluctantly trade their sexual favors for money or other douceurs. The homosexual slang use depends on the dictionary definition of trade as the process of buying, selling, or exchanging commodities, but it differs from it in denoting primarily persons rather than activities. Clearly in many cases the trade self-concept serves as a bridge to a reconstituted identity as a self-defining homosexual, hence the saying, "This year's trade is next year's competition." In other instances trade is essentially to be equated with hustling and may be a temporary behavior pattern. The existence of trade offers a continuing reservoir of sexual partners for those who do not want to trick with obvious gays, and who may even cherish the belief that they have sex only with straights.[9]

As a definition that maintains a signifying mobility, Dynes's entry effectively captures the overall spirit of "trade." Articulating the slang term's distinction from the traditional definition, it gestures toward commodity exchange while also stressing the capacity of the term to identify subjects who trade in sexual attention. Dynes also points to trade as that which connotes a temporary or transitional subject position. This position is unstable insofar as the identification of trade, self-imposed or otherwise, involves a visible performance of straight masculinity that is somehow in tension with imagined desires and practices not traditionally aligned with that identity. While trade connotes "primarily persons rather than activities," it indexes activities that are often projected possibilities for those bodies that signify as trade. In other words, a performance of straightness, however coded, conditions desire insofar as it also allows for some fantasy of or potential for homosexual contact on the part of those who desire trade.

From John Rechy's *City of Night* to Larry Clark's images of hustlers, a sign system of availability and threat has been well documented in literature and visual art that communicates a trade aesthetic. These records of desire map sexual practices and attire while also conveying an overall sensibility and providing a visual code that allows one to locate, read, and fantasize about the bodies of trade. They are as much pedagogical documents of desire as they are seductive narratives of queer urban contact.[10] Within this visual discursive field of desire, LA II comes to signify as trade. Until Times Square's 1990s rezoning, it had historically been a prime site for the exploration of trade; it continues to represent, however sparsely, a geography in which practices that threaten normative ideals of sexuality have been commodified and made available to those who wish to pursue a sexual life on the margins. Perhaps no writer has produced a more compelling documentary-based narrative of this sexual underworld than science-fiction writer Samuel Delany. His 1999 book *Times Square Red/Time Square Blue* further elaborates the world of New York City trade and details what I identify as a "john" subject position. I take a slight detour through Delany's narrative because his accounts of contact evoke the intricate and thorny ways of trade relationships. This critical departure paves a conceptual path to approach Haring's contact with trade and to clarify how LA II comes to occupy the role he does.

In *Times Square Red/Times Square Blue*, Delany argues that, within capitalism, life is at its most rewarding when individuals seek out and engage in interclass contact. Delany finds potential for a better life in the relations that occur in New York City's adult pornography theaters and other public sex spaces. *Times Square Red/Times Square Blue* offers a cultural commentary to support Delany's promotion of interclass contact as engendering a critical engagement with the discursive and systemic operations of capital. In the first section of the book, "Times Square Blue," Delany documents New York's disappearing public sex culture. Writing during Rudolph Giuliani's 1994–2001 reign as mayor, and toward the end of the mayor's expertly executed plan to "clean up" the city for increased business, Delany charts his experiences over thirty years of attending the adult theaters and hustler bars now under attack by the administration's "quality of life" campaign. With the declared goals of guaranteeing increased safety and a cleaner environment for city residents, countercultural spaces deemed a threat to family values and the good of society became direct targets. For Delany, the "cleaning up" of Times Square signifies a force of capital in which the potential for interclass connections and relations is greatly diminished. Delany's project provides an important critique of quality-of-life agendas and documents the valuable forms of contact that occur in public sex spaces, and the book has deservedly become a central reference point in queer studies, as a community of scholars and activists frustrated with the political climate of New York City have embraced the observations of a black queer man on the value of contact and community within alternative spaces of public sex. I also find Delany's text useful, but I am critical of his relationships to the individuals he documents. In an effort to highlight the potential of contact, Delany reveals the limitations of his own desire—a desire that frames itself as empathetic with the other but fails to take the measure of his own desire for these men and the role he plays in their objectification. This desire allows Delany meaningful relations without fully considering the men with whom he comes in contact.

Delany's projections and remembrances are clearly those of a john. In the framework of trade relationships, "john" indexes a positionality that—like trade—is not so clearly defined. The term can refer to a person who desires and seeks out relations without necessarily engaging in a straightforward monetary exchange. This desiring position, conditioned by sexual and commodity fetishism, is one of disavowal, in which trade's subjectivity is eclipsed, sometimes violently, by the projections of the john. "Times Square Blue" presents a narrative of john experience in which Delany's desire for an intimacy beyond crude economics engenders a rather troubling relationship to trade.

In the beginning of "Times Square Blue," Delany names two Times Square hustlers, Darrell Deckard and David Rosenbloom. These two figures act as human-interest anchors, grounding Delany's observations of the shifting landscape and systemic forces affecting Times Square in the experience of two individuals. Delany's discussion of Deckard and Rosenbloom is accompanied by photographic images of the two men. Delany discusses the moment in which one of the photographs was taken:

> While we set up our camera, Darrell and Dave mimed karate moves at one another and joked about the specific sexual services each

sold. At one point Darrell broke up. "Man, that nigger wants a hit of crack *so* bad. . . . I stopped smoking it, myself, last week. But that nigger"—meaning very white Dave—"will do *anything* for his hit!" Anything, here, meant sitting down to let himself be photographed too, for the fifteen dollars we offered him for his time and his signature on the model release. Then Dave was *gone!*[11]

What strikes me in the passage above is the liberty with which Delany names and photographs two men, calling attention not only to their hustling but also to their drug use. For a mere thirty dollars, Delany acquires signatures that allow him to reproduce images of these men, binding them to a formal system of visibility that increases their vulnerability to the very structures of policing he is critically marking. The condescendingly ethnographic tone of Delany's documentation is repeated throughout the section, where encounters with trade are documented and made visible for the reader. Indeed, despite his somewhat breezy tone, the frisson of excitement that radiates from this and other similar scenes in the book depends on the moralized framework around sex work that Delany's overt project is to dispute. One result is that the exchange of money takes on a certain air of prurience.

Philip-Lorca diCorcia, the photographer who took the pictures for Delany's book, has produced these images as more or less straightforward documentation to support Delany's text. But diCorcia became well known in the early 1990s for his Hustlers series, a set of images that played self-consciously with images of male sex workers promoted by artists like Larry Clark. For this project diCorcia would set up the shot and leave his assistant to monitor his equipment while he found men on the streets in West Hollywood to pose for him. In exchange, he would give them a small portion of the National Endowment for the Arts grant he had received to fund the project. DiCorcia undertook the Hustlers project in the immediate aftermath of the "NEA Four" controversy, the 1990 event in which Congress withdrew funding from artists (Robert Mapplethorpe, Tim Miller, Holly Hughes, and John Fleck) due to charges of obscenity; as a result, diCorcia's grant was conditional on him signing an agreement stating that he would not produce any obscene imagery with his money. The images, some more sexually explicit than others, evoke an erotics of trade that might not be legible as such to a larger mainstream audience. The sexual narratives suggested by the carefully crafted shots are more available to those familiar with the landscapes of queer sex. Under each photograph in the series, diCorcia lists the name given by each subject, the town in which they were born, and the amount of money he paid them to pose.[12] These subjects are not necessarily trading sex for money, but the constructed nature of the imagery renders these images potent investigations into the fantasies implicit in the scene of trade. DiCorcia's project foregrounds questions of the visuality of trade and the issue of agency in both the monetary and photographic exchange. Delany's project has a different logic. He displays his intimate knowledge of a Times Square sexual economy and shows off an apparently instinctive ability to converse with hustlers and learn about their lives. But the meaningful sets of exchanges he claims and documents are dependent on an ethically fraught relationship with subjects that is never fully explored. Delany's personal desires eclipse any counter-commentary that would consider the needs of his "informants" beyond what he deems is in their interest.

While Delany's account of the Times Square theaters focuses on the socially advantageous potentials of contact, he does report one exceptional incident of violence. Claiming that he rarely felt in any great danger in the porn theaters, Delany nonetheless describes the actions of pickpockets:

> In the early years, if you fell asleep in the movies (as was fairly common once you shot your load, especially if you brought in a six pack of beer, a hip flask of wine, or a bottle of vodka), you could wake to find your hip pants pockets slit with a razor and your change gone or your wallet empty on the seat beside you. Many times when I saw one of the slash artists sliding in beside a snoozing patron, I'd go into the row behind, reach over and jog the sleeper's shoulder till he woke up—while the razor man got up, snarled at me, and fled.[13]

Delany goes on to describe being punched by someone who recognized him as the "guy who keeps waking everybody up." According to Delany, this was the only retaliation he experienced because of his good deeds. I find little distinction between Delany's moral imperative to protect the pockets of his fellow audience members and the moral framework underlying the redevelopment of Times Square that he wishes to criticize. The second-person voice by means of which the text projects an experience onto the reader signals Delany's own identification with the men in the audience who are at risk for theft. If we are to understand redevelopment's tie to family values as a call to make safe public space for a projected ideal of the self in a capitalist society—a self that stands counter to sexual deviants and criminals—Delany's projection of his self onto those men in the audience engenders a similar moral response.

That Delany marks the theft of money as an exceptional danger in the erotic space of interclass contact exemplifies not only john subjectivity but also the way in which trade as an object of desire is often denied care through the very operations of desire. Delany devotes a significant portion of his narrative to a hustler named Joey. Joey, once a hot commodity in the hustler bars, experiences a downward spiral and eventually earns the nickname "Joey-who-needs-a-bath." At this point Delany begins a regular exchange of money for sexual encounters with Joey. But after a few weeks, Delany does not appear for a scheduled meeting. Despite the captivating sexual self-confidence Joey possessed, Delany writes that "hustlers are just not my particular thing."[14] This sentiment (and the verbal formula) is echoed pages later in a discussion of go-go dancers. "After performing on stage," Delany writes, "male dancers came out to walk the aisles and hustle the audience . . . but for me the whole thing was too mercenary, too formalized, and—like hustlers—go-go dancers in general aren't my thing."[15] The exchanges Delany prefers are more missionary than mercenary: in the theater, he buys men things like soft drinks and sandwiches. For Delany, the most rewarding exchanges involve not money but the opportunity to project his own notion of what the other needs. In this way, his romantic interclass contact can remain unsullied by the money he pointedly wants to protect, making every effort he can to prevent its visibility within the space of the theater. Offering goods instead of money, Delany limits the possibility for trade in its fullest sense—limits, that is, the possibility for these men to make decisions for themselves as to what they need. This, no less than the actions of pickpockets, constitutes its own form of violence.

While I think the theoretical potentials of interclass contact as offered by Delany in the second half of *Times Square Red/Times Square Blue* are compromised by the workings of the first half of the book, I do not mean to dismiss Delany's experience. As a subjective memoir of contact, it communicates an engaging and emotional tie to public sex spaces. What Delany's text allows me to consider is how trade offers meaningful contact even as the men designated as trade are denied access to forms of support that fail to fit with the fantasies of the men who desire them. Highlighting the queer economy of trade and john in Delany's work, one in which moments of queer possibility are continually bound to capitalism and the protection of money, points to a system of contact and engagement useful in understanding Haring's relationship to LA II.

Portrait of the Artist as a Young John

By both artists' accounts, Haring's and LA II's collaboration was mutually beneficial and enriching. But these men produced their work in an economy of authenticity and prestige that fundamentally inflected how their coproduction was perceived. The younger artist became a key signifier for arts writers and consumers interested in Haring's connection to hip-hop communities. Both the tag LA II, and the boy behind it, circulated as signs of authenticity that came to enhance Haring's own line and furthered a popular interest in Haring's versatility as an artist. The young, often shirtless brown subject at Haring's side functioned as a fetish object for an art market invested in the aura of the street. In the world of trade, even the suggestion of sexual possibilities between men generates desire for those who learn to read availability in trade's aesthetic codes of straight masculinity. Complementary to this, the john also becomes a signifier of want, a symbol of potential activities that may never actually occur. Like trade, the role of john is a mobile, transitory, and unfixed position. Haring and LA II profited from a coded system of visibility, where the desire for both white privilege and contact with a creative, racialized underclass informed the homosocial bond between the young gay artist and the straight-identified Puerto Rican teenager. Trade aesthetics is a framework for thinking through the visual discursive field that both artists come to occupy in the press and the reception of the work they create together. If LA II projects the well-established visual cues of Puerto Rican trade, then Haring as a visual counterpoint might be seen as akin to a john in his eager embrace of LA II. In framing them this way, I aim not to divine some truth about their sexual life but to read their documented exchange as a cultural text, where trade and john archetypes signal the larger structural conditions of cross-racial desire with which Haring and LA II contended. Haring's impulse toward that which is authentically connected to black and Latinx forms of expression is bound up with an erotically charged sphere of contact, in which Haring mediates between those interested in his art and the brown bodies that inspire him.

In a 1990 essay entitled "New York Reflections," the sociologist Richard Sennett describes a Tseng Kwong Chi photograph of LA II and Haring reproduced in a 1983 catalog for Sidney Janis Gallery's *Post-Graffiti* exhibition. Sennett renders the photograph in the following terms, exemplifying how the brown flesh of LA II often signifies in relationship to Haring:

> In the catalogue of this show, there is a photograph of Keith Haring, a young white artist who adapted graffiti writing to a tamer scribbling which can decorate posters and T-shirts as well as canvas. In the photo he is wearing one of these mass-produced Keith Haring T-shirts. Next to him is a dark Puerto Rican young man wearing nothing but a cross on a string and a pair of boxer shorts, his nipples like black buttons on brown skin; he is Angel Ortiz, widely known on the subways as L.A. II. Just as the clothed white artist is advertising his clothes, so the nakedness of the slum Hispanic is an advertisement.[16]

In an essay grappling with the subjective experiences of people encountering difference in New York City, Sennett might be sardonically mapping a white bourgeois sensibility onto the image, but the intensity with which he focuses on LA II's flesh is remarkable. In the absence of a shirt, LA II's nipples become something like an accessory to complement his boxer shorts and the cross dangling around his neck. Sennett reads brown into a black-and-white image and describes LA II through an aesthetic mapping of difference. In Sennett's account, Haring's commodity clothing stands in stark contrast to the fetishized "buttons" of LA II's nipples, a contrast that both recognizes and repeats the fantasy of brownness as constituting its own fleshy clothing. Against Haring's "tamer scribbling," the radiant baby that appears across his clothed chest, LA II's dark buttons of flesh are their own commodity, metonymically tying the body of the graffiti artist to an imagined culture of the slum.

Sennett frames the visual economy of cross-racial contact in exaggeratedly racialized terms, even as he astutely positions Haring and LA II within the cultural moment in which graffiti became part of a gallery landscape. Discussing how graffiti was seen as something criminal to be controlled by the state, Sennett argues that the lines of graffiti are aggressive acts that "force others to respond to the presence of the juvenile underclass, declaring itself."[17] Sennett quotes (without naming the quotation's provenance) a notorious statement by Harvard sociologist Nathan Glazer to demonstrate how the presence of graffiti inspired fear. As Glazer's 1979 essay "On Subway Graffiti in New York" had put it, "While I do not find myself consciously making the connection between the graffiti-makers and the criminals who occasionally rob, rape and assault passengers, the sense that all are part of one world of uncontrollable predators seems inescapable."[18] For Glazer, the marks of graffiti, as the visible evidence of an imagined criminal class, imbue the subway with a sense of danger, and this is what the control of graffiti helps mitigate. Sennett understands the post-graffiti art movement, and the recognition of LA II in particular, as another form of control that lessened what he refers to as "the sting" of difference embodied by graffiti. The elevation of the graffiti artist, argues Sennett, represents another mode of captivity in which the fear of difference is commodified through the language of appreciation.

In the *Post-Graffiti* catalog, the following quotation from Haring is printed below the image that captures Sennett's attention: "Because he possesses qualities that are uniquely human, the image maker, in the history of man, may be more important now than at any other time . . . his imagination is our greatest hope for survival."[19] Invoking a universalizing frame of reference, Haring's words illuminate precisely Sennett's claims about the containing effect of graffiti's transplantation to the gallery. But those words also hauntingly and ironically highlight the persistent race and class dynamics that would inform the terms of LA II's visibility after Haring's death.

In 1990, the *Village Voice* dedicated a special memorial section to Haring that included an article about LA II. The story exemplifies the kind of racist imaginings with which LA II had to contend and demonstrates the trade role he inhabited in his relationship with Haring. In "Tag Team: LA II Remembers the Guy Who 'Draws Babies on the Door,'" Katherine Dieckmann discusses a visit with LA II. She draws readers into the story by describing a photograph from 1982 (one from the shoot that produced the image discussed by Sennett) (figure 2.1). In a detailed reading of the image, Dieckmann pulls together the visual elements of this captured moment to assert a particular narrative about Haring, LA II, and Tseng:

> Here's a photograph of two young men. One of them, a boy of 15, is bare-chested and wearing gym shorts. Bent on one knee, he's rubbing his hands together. His skin is dark. He looks happy. Beside him squats a white man in his early twenties. He's wearing nerdy glasses. He looks relaxed. All around them, on the white floor and wall, are black shapes and squiggles—some recognizable as running and crawling figures, some as graffito markings, all sharp angles and wild swirls. What you notice in this picture isn't the wraparound artwork, but the expression on the faces of the two young men in

Figure 2.1. Keith Haring and LA II in front of their collaboration, 1982. Photo by Tseng Kwong Chi © Muna Tseng Dance Projects, Inc., www.tsengkwongchi.com. Art by Keith Haring © The Keith Haring Foundation.

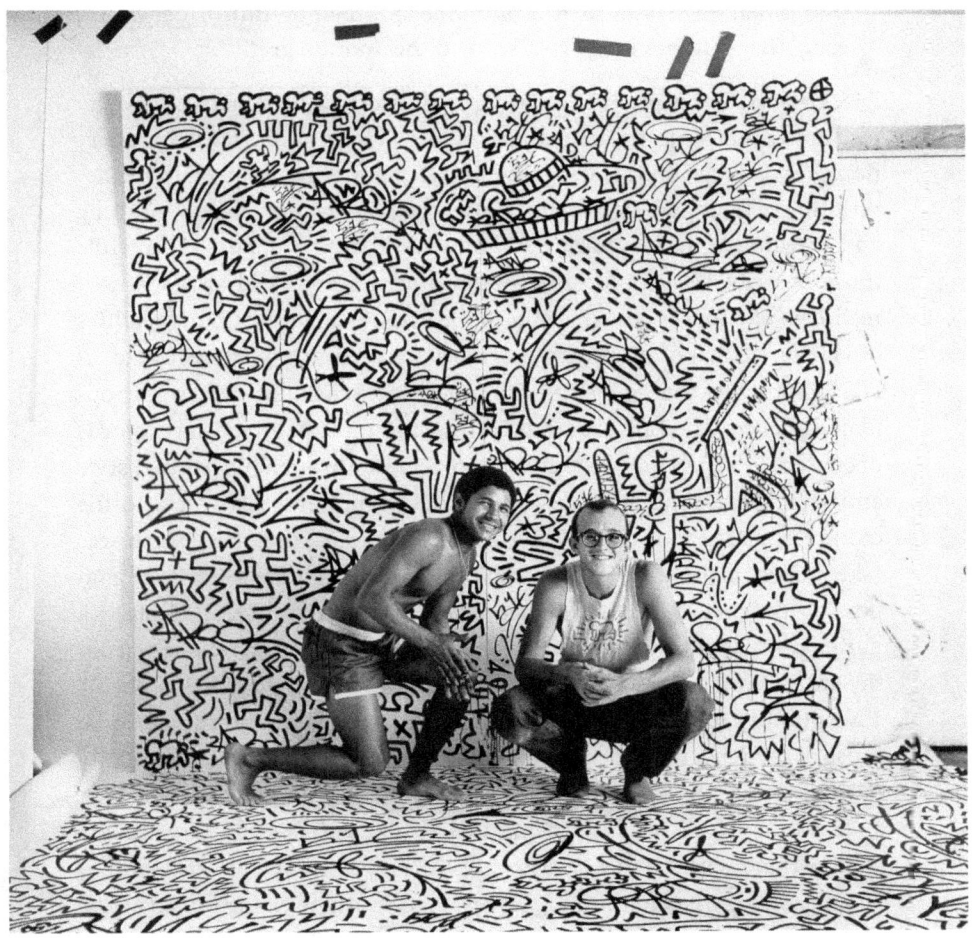

front of it. They are beaming at the photographer as radiant as the baby printed on the white man's tank top.

The narrative continues:

> Today, the older man, Keith Haring, is dead of AIDS. So is the Chinese man who took the picture, Tseng Kwong Chi. Back in '82, one might have wagered that it was the Puerto Rican kid from the Lower East Side who might be wiped out at an early age from drugs or violence—certainly not the white, middle-class guy by his side. But Angel Ortiz, better known by his tag LA II, is still alive. He's 23 now, and he's taciturn until he starts to trust you. Then glimmers of sweet warmth flicker beneath his brusque exterior. He smiles now and then, but not as openly as in Kwong Chi's picture. And he says things that might seem a little outmoded for their optimism, considering that galleries long ago slammed the door on graffiti.[20]

Dieckmann's description engages with the erotics of contact and spectatorship so central to the consumption of Haring's neoprimitive production. Her piece fashions Haring into a kind of pop ethnographer. In her description of lines and their forms, those which are recognizable—running and crawling figures—appear to align with Haring's line drawing, while those described as graffito lines—sharp angles and wild swirls—more readily evoke LA II's contribution to the artwork. The economic realities of Haring's collaboration with LA II are made painfully evident here, as Haring provides the legible conditions for LA II's visibility to a larger popular audience. The canvases that Haring and LA II paint exist as records of contact in which the white cultural producer, through his popular style and established language of communication, presents his access to the culture of a Latino youth. In 1990, eight years after the photograph was taken, Dieckmann encounters a subject who at first reads as resistant and possibly threatening but who then opens up to his interviewer and shares a naïve optimism not quite in line with the times. The narrative works from the author's own stereotyped presumptions about her subject's probable susceptibility to urban danger; these presumptions are presumed to be those of her readers, who are invited to "speculate" on the likely longevity of these differently vulnerable bodies.

Dieckmann's article also paints a particular portrait of desire and exchange that focuses on LA II's sexuality, his access to the gay lifeworld of Haring, and the economic gains of his relationship with the famed artist.

At one point in the article, Dieckmann describes a project in which LA II and Haring tagged a statue of a female bust that had been painted in Day-Glo colors. This particular art object occasions Dieckmann's discussion of LA II's discomfort with Haring's sexuality:

> Smothering statues of women with doodles wasn't a big part of Haring's repertoire, except for his work with LA. It was Haring who would pick out what they would paint on, explains LA. The choice of subject matter may or may not have had something to do with the fact that, unlike many of the black and Hispanic youths Haring befriended over the years, LA was straight. "Keith would take me to the Paradise Garage with him, but I wasn't into that crowd," LA says, a little uncomfortable. "I wasn't raised with gay stuff and all of that. I didn't have nothing against them, but it was hard for me at first." For one thing, many of his friends accused him of making his money by sleeping with Keith. "And I'd say, 'No, it's not like that. He shows me respect. I show him respect. We're both men.'"[21]

Dieckmann's suggestions that an inanimate female bust would be Haring's concession to LA II's heterosexuality represents an absurd and willful inability to think differently, which is to say, perhaps, queerly, around the erotic field of exchange that energizes their artistic coupling. At the same time, LA II's own discourse about his discomfort around Haring's queer crowd produces the very fantasy of trade as a straight-identified man who, despite this initial discomfort, appreciates and respects his partner and continues to hang out in the gay social spheres that afford him increased access to cultural and financial capital. In some ways, the assertion of heterosexuality points to an insecurity that is an effect of the emasculated trade position where Haring's class and race privilege engender a scene of patronage, which reproduces a hetero-patriarchal structure of exploitation; Tseng Kwong Chi's portrait reflects a field of uneven privilege that in turn facilitates an insidious, racist, heteronormative gaze. How might a focus on the exchange between artists at the level of the line, however, reveal a less predictable story around the effects of white appropriation?

Radiant Trade

The afterlife of Haring's relationship with LA II appears more recently in the *Village Voice*, in which LA II directly confronts the economic fallout of his unprotected role as a contributor to Haring's art. Rather than simply reproducing the seductive pull of an exploitation narrative—a discursive project that itself engenders a patronizing relationship to LA II even as it criticizes the institutional disregard for the graffiti artist—I explore the scenes in which LA II's painted line appears in an attempt to highlight its animating capacity in a scene of complicity that cannot be reduced to a pious critique of whiteness. This move to the line suggests how a trade figure like LA II might navigate his own desire within the structure of artistic and cultural exchange.

Eleven years after Dieckmann's story appeared, the *Voice* ran another feature on LA II. While his relationship to Haring was once again central to his publicity, the stakes of his claims were decidedly different. In the 2002 piece "Keith Haring's Silent Partner," *Voice* columnist Colin Moynihan profiles a thirty-five-year-old LA II and discusses his developing friendship with Haring, including the original moment of collaboration in which the two painted a detached metal section of a taxi cab hood that eventually sold for $1,400. Haring gave LA II half of this sum. Moynihan provides a pointed commentary on the workings of the Haring Foundation, claiming that it refused proper recognition to LA II, thereby denying him exposure and monetary gain for work in which he was directly involved. Moynihan presents a melancholic narrative in which Haring's absence conditions the lack of appropriate recognition and monetary support:

> It is not only the potential loss of money but also the lack of acknowledgement that pains Ortiz. He thought of Haring not merely as a business partner, but as a trusted friend and supporter who plucked him from obscurity, encouraged him to create art, and invited him to share in an adventure. The fact that the Haring Foundation appears to prefer keeping him at arm's length puzzles Ortiz and makes him miss all the more the reassuring presence of his former mentor.
>
> "The foundation should've taken care of me, but they didn't," he said.[22]

Dubious about the sentimentality of the narrative Moynihan produces, I am affected by that final statement. As trade, LA II could be seen as an inspiration and source of the street's authentic "spirit and soul," but it seems that the terms of his production with Haring cannot be contractually recognized in such a way as to ensure ongoing access to potential profits from their coproduced work.

Moynihan's article appeared in the wake of an exhibition that opened in late June 2002 in Manhattan's Lower East Side. The postcard announcement for the opening shows a *Museums New York* magazine cover in which a large vase appears below Keith Haring's name. Haring's trademarks—a radiant baby, a glowing pyramid, and outline figures of dancing men—adorn the object. Within and around these figures appear markings produced by LA II. The postcard asks the questions, "What is wrong with this picture?," "Can you spot the error?," and "Where is LA II?" The show, entitled *Setting the Record Straight*, attempted to make people aware of LA II's unrecognized contributions to Haring's work while also allowing viewers to see the Latino artist's continuing creativity and production. At a moment when the Keith Haring Foundation refused to attend properly to LA II as a contributor, *Setting the Record Straight* generated a new buzz around LA II and brought art collectors in contact, once again, with a graffiti culture that had fallen out of fashion with the art market. With *Setting the Record Straight*, the graffiti artist displayed a style and movement of line that renewed capital interest in his work. Continuing to work on solo projects and collaborations with well-established artists, such as Marco and Paul Kostabi, LA II had found gallery representation in an art market once again interested in 1980s aesthetic practices.

But the postcard's call to "set the record straight" not only referenced the truth of LA II's contribution; it also read as an aggressive statement against Haring's publicly acknowledged homosexuality. Haring has become memorialized and institutionalized as a gay artist. To set the record straight, LA II is framed as a heterosexual Latino producing work on his own terms. His official visibility in the collaborations with Haring becomes tied to his insertion within a masculine, heterosexual world of hip-hop. This form of acknowledging the material conditions and problematic workings of Haring and LA II's relationship risks losing sight of the queer potential in the trade negotiations between these two artists. What becomes clear, however, in the continual assertion of LA II's heterosexuality is an inability to escape the terms of the trade/john relationship. In validating LA II as a dismissed contributor, the press surrounding LA II's more recent work reinserts him into the trade position. His outwardly claimed heterosexuality is in many ways a necessary part of the original field of erotic fantasy, and the continued performance of his heterosexuality sustains that volatile space of availability and threat. This strategy for recuperating and validating LA II's contribution relies on, without acknowledging, the queerness of trade. But that queerness is palpable even, or especially, in LA II's assertions of heterosexuality: in recounting the nonreciprocity of desire between him and Haring, LA II subtly evokes the queer economy that brought him wide visibility in his youth and continues to seduce prospective buyers with a trade erotics of the street.

Those erotics complicate notions of straightforwardly static relationships of power; attending to them restores some of the complexity of the agency of the person occupying the role of trade as well as that of the john. One of the most searching explorations of such dynamics in the context of race and queer desire is offered in Frances Negrón-Muntaner's book *Boricua Pop: Puerto Ricans and the Latinization of American Culture.* Moving from *West Side Story* to Ricky Martin, Negrón-Muntaner calls attention to the ways in which Puerto Ricans have made invaluable contributions to American pop culture while navigating racist systems of repression and objectification. Her consideration of the 1980s art market contrasts Haring to the figure of Jean-Michel Basquiat. For Negrón-Muntaner, Basquiat's racialized character was a source of fascination for the market but also created forms of resistance that prevented his work from being easily consumed. Haring, by contrast, was able to mobilize his queerness to access a racialized street culture. She writes, "If as a queer man, Haring had to contend with the shame of gay identity and the homophobia of compulsory heterosexual culture, his privileged ethnic identification and de-racializing queerness allowed for the appropriation of graffiti practices in ways that graffiti writers themselves were unable to do and racialized artists like Basquiat were afraid to."[23]

Negrón-Muntaner's observations about the "de-racializing" effects of Haring's public persona are trenchant. But they also tend to simplify the queerness of the trade relations Haring established with his lovers and collaborators. The passage continues: "Haring particularly liked the Puerto Rican 'toughs' who, if gay, catered to his fantasies and assured him of his superiority by staying at home and cooking for him, or if straight, allowed him to serve as a 'father' or older brother figure."[24] Her criticism references many of the problematic statements made by Haring and his contemporaries about Juan Dubose that I discuss in the introduction. For example, Bruno and Carmel Schmidt, friends of Haring from his days at SVA, paint Dubose as a "nagging wife"—a portrait apparently buttressed by what Gruen's biography presents as Haring's need to break up with Dubose, be less domestic, and live as a bachelor.[25]

But the narratives produced around Haring's proclivity for Puerto Rican boys can be perhaps better understood in terms of a discursive formulation of trade than within limited heterosexual tropes of subjection. The language of trade helps us see the ways in which Haring can never maintain normative relationships. The moments of greatest contention with his Puerto Rican lovers come at times when trade fails to deliver the kind of relationship Haring desires. How might an active investment in the domestic sphere and private property be a means for "a piece of trade" to assert himself against Haring's projected needs? If Haring senses an internal nonwhiteness that might assuage his implication in a history of violent subjection, what happens when trade acts out in such a way as to reinforce a master/domestic servant relationship rather than allowing for a feeling of union and equality? The fraternal and domestic classifications Negrón-Muntaner criticizes should not be understood as simple reproductions of heterosexual roles or ones that are inhabited solely for the pleasure of the john.

Trade engenders a difficult and ambiguous relationship. In my analysis of trade as a specifically queer set of relations that resists straightforward readings of economic and cultural exchange, I want to extend Negrón-Muntaner's discussion to stress the volatility of agency in the scene of trade. This volatility is visible not only in the ways we discuss Haring's life but in the surfaces of his art—perhaps in particular his collaborative work. I want to turn in closing to a particularly striking instance of that collaboration, an untitled canvas from 1982 that signals a new expansiveness of line in Haring's work. LA II's influence in this development is literally written into this canvas: his tags "LA II" and "LA ROCK" appear in various sizes within and around the flying saucers, barking dogs, pyramids, and radiant babies that crowd the canvas. In addition, LA II's signature curved arrows, which point in multiple directions, engender a dizzying movement that distracts from Haring's easily consumed figures, as if in a kind of competition for the viewer's attention. The marks and lines that populate much of the canvas aggressively surround, enter, and engage Haring's forms—with the result that even Haring's supremely recognizable forms become harder to see in the crowded and flattened plane. The pivotal role of the canvas has been signaled by the Haring Foundation's executive director Julia Gruen, who references it in an online essay for the foundation's website that traces "the changes and developments in Keith's approach to pattern."[26]

Those changes need to be understood in terms of Haring's relations—transactional in the most ample sense—with men of color. In staging the interpenetration of Haring's and LA II's lines, the surfaces on which these artists left their mark can be seen as formal indexes of Haring's understanding of race and his desire to become something other than white. But his forms also evoke the limits of whiteness, their bounded bodies inhabited and surrounded by LA II's signature. This artistic exchange is a scene of possibility and frustration: Haring's contact with a Puerto Rican youth is recorded, even as his figures thereby become in one sense more rather than less fully racialized, as Haring's outlines contend with LA II's tags and so become more sharply differentiated. And yet, the intensity and aggressiveness of LA II's line speak to the complexity of that contact and the desire that provoked it. The site is a navigation of difference, both intimate and forceful, that cannot be separated from cross-racial desire, the kind of possibility that desire produces, and the seductive energy of trade. LA II's expansive tagging both eclipses and magnifies Haring's work as it distracts from the form but never goes so far as to erase the aesthetic that is key to the work's lucrative status.

The idea of trade I elaborate here understands this as a radiant relationship—if we understand radiance not as a sentimentalized glow that shines off perfect communion but as the politically and aesthetically ambivalent energy that pulses from and as a line produced in the friction of complicity, desire, and inequality. Haring's line—produced in part with and against LA II's—is a testament to the radiance of trade in this sense. It is a product and a sign of a relation in which appropriation is impossible to disentangle from the movement of the erotic and the play of power. LA II may have understood the economics of his collaboration with Haring, but no official system was set up to recognize his work, and that omission allows for the romanticization of Haring's exchange with an authentic racially marked street culture he famously mined for inspiration. But to participate in that romanticization is also to ignore what is most queer in this relationship, which is still not fully recognized within the normative legal structures that protect property rights. For now, the complexity of that relationship is best recognized in the works, those crossed lines, that still radiate with their complicitous connection.

In Grace Jones's 1986 music video "I'm Not Perfect (But I'm Perfect for You)," she appears in faux-primitive drag, which includes a fiery headdress of vivid orange, red, and yellow (figure 3.1). Wiry, bright threads emerge from the back of her neck and head, streaming down the length of her torso. Enclosing her breasts, two red cones jut forth in a spiral pattern, their ends draped with a mass of long, stringy material that sways with the flow of her bodily movement. The centerpiece of her costume extends from the lower half of her body and effects an exaggerated height that places Jones in a scale beyond Amazonian proportions. The skirt—sixty

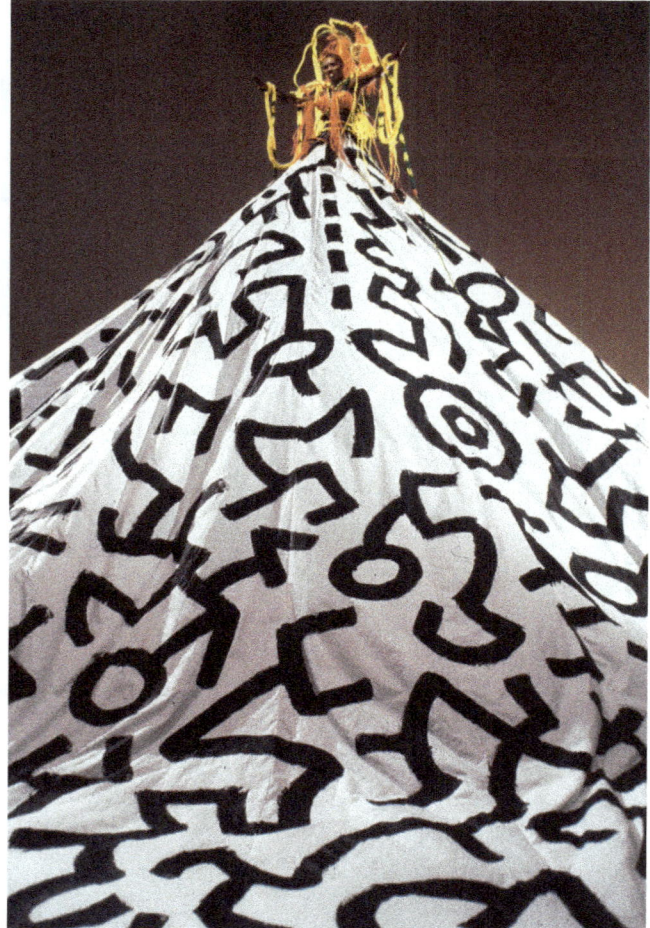

feet in diameter—billows outward, its white surface teeming with Haring's neoprimitive signs.

The narrative of the video involves Jones's submission to practices of self-care that appear more as sites of subjection than they do healing or beneficial exercises. Jones undergoes mud masks, painful hot-wax treatments for the removal of hair, acupuncture to combat aging around the eyes, aggressive massage therapy, submersion in a tub filled with milk, and

Figure 3.1. Grace Jones in Haring-painted skirt in "I'm Not Perfect (But I'm Perfect for You)" music video, 1986. Photo by Tseng Kwong Chi © Muna Tseng Dance Projects, Inc., www.tsengkwongchi.com. Art by Keith Haring © The Keith Haring Foundation.

an excruciating psychotherapy session. The treatments are administered by sinister figures, as Jones appears tense and panicked throughout the processing of her body. Interspersed with these scenes, various individuals attest to Jones's charms. At one moment, Andy Warhol appears and says with his signature blasé enthusiasm, "Grace is perfect."[1]

On one level, the video (the only one Jones directed herself) appears as a humorous reading of perfection and the lengths one must go to in order to achieve a stellar appearance for consuming audiences. And yet, an alternate thread occurs—made available through the aggressive power of Jones's performance—in which the fantasy of the primitive acts as a site of possibility, a potential beyond the subjection to perfection. Juxtaposed with the scenes of torturous care are ones of Jones dancing in primitive gear in front of a mass of writhing bodies. In these scenes, Jones poses wild-eyed, with her mouth open. Here, she performs as a primal figure of blackness and strength in opposition to the subjugated pose she strikes in the other scenes. Toward the end of the video, Jones casts out her bright threads, ensnaring the therapists who have caused her such discomfort on the path to perfection. In the final scene, the masses of dancing bodies become subsumed under the flowing white skirt produced by Haring. The thriving mass is incorporated into the grand image of Grace Jones as fierce performer and energetic spiritual icon. Discussing Jones's idea for the costume, Haring stated, "She's going to be like the Pied Piper, and she'd be singing and all these people are following her and they go underneath the skirt, and the skirt consumes them as Grace floats away into the sky."[2]

At the end of the video, Jones is a figure of grotesque proportions, not in her physical form but in the excessive extensions attached to her body—Haring's enormous skirt and the accoutrements that adorn her form. She is a pop-primitive explosion. The very articles that come to frame this primitive diva in motion become the tools to entangle and ensnare those who have manipulated her body into perfection, as the writhing mass of bodies that celebrate this constructed beast are consumed by the skirt. Haring's artistic work swallows the idolizing mass, and Jones is elevated above it; the produced image of primitive possibility consumes both producers and audience as Jones transcends all. "I'm Not Perfect" presents a narrative of performance production that mirrors Jones's own relationship to the structures of her visibility and the productions of excess that become her iconography. Those who claim to mold her are entranced by her rhythm, becoming swallowed in the ever-increasing mass of signifiers, as they try to keep up to the beat of this Pied Piper.

The music video, with its refrain "I'm not perfect, but I'm perfect for you" captures something of Jones's celebrated difficulty as a supposed diva while also indicating how her image and the draw of her black body are indeed the perfect inspiration for white male artists to enact their fetishistic fantasies. While the narrative suggests that Jones must undergo processes of manipulation to achieve a perfection that would be recognized by figures such as Warhol, it could also suggest that Jones always inhabits perfection for these figures. She is perfect for their assessment and idealization, and the chic trends in self-care become superfluous to her very existence, which is to say, she is the perfect figure for their ideas of perfection. In the refrain, she authors herself toward the authorial tendencies of these cultural producers who desire her perfection.

The video is emblematic of Jones's relationship to the world of image production she inhabits at the height of 1980s glamour. The processing of her body via fashionable forms of self-care reverberates with French photographer and graphic designer Jean-Paul Goude's manipulation of Jones's flesh in imagery that came to define her aesthetic throughout the decade. In this chapter, I look to the vexed relationship between Jones and Goude (whose intimate relationship lasted from 1977 to the end of the decade and resulted in a son), exploring how Jones's body had been written out as a fantasy of blackness that later came to inspire Haring's own visual manipulations of her form through his line. Goude insisted on enhancing Jones's body toward an ideal of primitive beauty. Jones's real flesh, while inspiring to Goude, must be refashioned to fit a project in which her blackness is hyperaestheticized and achieves, in his formulation, a more perfect reflection of the modern black woman Jones purportedly is.

Jones's experience in New York nightclubs prior to, during, and beyond her collaborations with Goude were experiments in sound and movement that reflected the political climate of creativity in which she was submerged, particularly that of the underground gay clubs that both inspired her and provided her with eager audiences. During the mid 1980s, Yale art historian Robert Farris Thompson was invited by Haring to photograph the painting of Jones's body at one such club, New York's Paradise Garage. This experience led Thompson (who had invited Haring to lecture to his classes and was one of the first scholars to write about Haring's art) to describe Grace Jones as Haring's "theory . . . made flesh."[3] Following Jones's career prior to and after meeting Haring, this chapter ends at the Paradise Garage, with an examination of archival video footage of Jones performing there in 1985 wearing Haring's lines—a scene in which, according to an insightful analysis by Miriam Kershaw, Jones was "transformed into a power site."[4] Thompson's provocative assessment of Grace Jones, one that imagines her as the physical embodiment of the concepts represented by Haring's line, drives the central question of this chapter: What does it mean to imagine Jones as theory made flesh, as the enfleshment of Haring's neoprimitive line? Echoing the introductory scene of this book, I am concerned with Haring's line as it emerges on the flesh of the black performer. The drama of Haring's line—with its complex evocations of the primitive and the universal—asserts itself against Jones's body, and, as with Bill T. Jones, could be understood as animating a scene of becoming primitive for Grace Jones.

But this chapter seeks to make visible how Jones's performances—and her account of them—complicate any notion of theory's separability from flesh. Although it makes a certain kind of sense to note that Jones's body arrives under Haring's brush after already having been treated by Goude's manipulations, this narrative still suggests that Jones's flesh is the raw material for white male theorization. The accounts Jones offers are more complex: they indicate her awareness of the impossibility of rescuing a prediscursive truth of black flesh and her excited sense of complicity in the making of the Grace Jones myth, even from within the scenarios of racist fantasy and desiring projection that set the terms for that myth. In thinking through the complexity of Jones's performance of embodiment, I have been inspired by the work of critical race theorist Rey Chow; her argument about the condition of the ethnic as one of captivity has been useful in thinking about the scripts written onto and through Jones's body within a predictable spectacle of black primitivism.[5] But while Chow's theory of entrapment provides one way to consider Jones's body as theory made flesh, I am also interested in the conceptual logic developed by Gilles Deleuze and Félix Guattari, particularly their key notions of deterritorialization and lines of flight. Like Chow, these theorists understand the immobilizing force that identity narratives impose on bodies, but they also provide a way to imagine a constantly animating potential in the very networks that come to contain and make something like desire legible.[6] In the conclusion to this chapter, I literalize the concept of lines of flight to imagine what might be happening as Grace Jones takes to the stage at the Paradise Garage, animating Haring's lines in a visual and sonic field that in turn animates its audience to ecstatic heights.

Underground and in the Margins: Transformational Energies

In Rosa von Praunheim's *Army of Lovers, or, Revolt of the Perverts*, a 1979 documentary that investigates the state of gay and lesbian politics in the United States a decade after Stonewall, the German filmmaker interviews a lesbian separatist activist who is enraged that Grace Jones performed as part of a 1978 gay rights rally in New York City. The film shows Jones dancing under red stage lights and within the haze of a fog-machine cloud. At one moment a man appears on stage with her, joyfully dancing, and then the film cuts to a group of women and men in the audience gyrating to the music with hands in the air. Rather than sync the sound of the performance with the action on stage, von Praunheim layers the audio track of his conversation with the activist over the scene. "Gay men are so intrigued by role playing," says the filmmaker, "wanting to be more straight and more masculine than heterosexual men and . . . they see women as caricatures, as sex objects in a way, a kind of ugly way, and I see it myself, like today with Grace Jones, I was intrigued by her." "It's not that I blame you for being intrigued by her," the interviewee responds and continues to explain her position:

> You're a man first of all, and you're conditioned to feel that a woman is there for your pleasure. . . . It sort of feeds into your male pride that she's doing this for you, doing this to, what, make you feel good sexually? . . . I was horrified, I was absolutely livid. I was in a rage. . . . I felt like I was at a smoker of straight men who had a prostitute, hustler, whatever word you'd like to use, pop out of a cake to do some sexual gyration so they can get their rocks off. . . . It's very contemptuous of her. I hear some remarks, "She's a bitch!" and "She's this, that, and the other," and people applauded her at the same time. So it's a kind of a contradiction in terms. They want her to do this terrible thing to herself, and they hate her for doing it. Gay men are just like straight men. . . . That woman Grace Jones should not have been on that stage, should not have been permitted to set foot on that stage. She insulted every woman that was there. And that's what men like. They like to insult women.[7]

In a brilliant editing move, von Praunheim performs an earnest spoken investigation into his socially conditioned misogyny and allows his interviewee to speak over the image of Jones. The performance footage, with its representation of movement, style, and pleasure, does indeed intrigue. The affective energy of the footage, which shows what appears to be a multigendered audience enthusiastically engaging each other and Jones in a scene of rosy-hued pleasure, starkly counters the affective energy of rage, disgust, and offense being described on the soundtrack. While the footage might evidence the intriguing draw of Grace Jones, it also evidences something deeply unresolved and in excess of the binary gendered logic of male objectification that is being spoken. Grace Jones, in what has been her trademark since the beginning of her career, performs against gendered expectation. Even without sound, one can see that this figure hardly personifies a traditionally feminine presentation of self. The tension between what is being spoken and what is visually projected does not necessarily negate the critique forwarded—much of what this activist describes about gay men's misogyny rings true—but her analysis seems inadequate to the scene of pleasure. She seeks to make sense of men's vile behavior through social conditioning, but she places a particular kind of blame on Jones for daring to appear on the stage in front of men. This feminist reproach against Jones and the gay men who act "just like straight men" exemplifies the often limiting discourse of women's oppression that tends to universalize gender positions without any attention to the complexities of race and the multilayered signifying capacities of Jones in performance.

Anyone who follows Jones—and the various ways people make sense of her—knows that she is continually having to perform within and against intense scenes of social formation and political desire. Grace Jones's body seems always to be on the line in deep scenes of historical and political transformation—transformations fueled explicitly by desire and sexual contact. Describing the gay dance clubs of 1970s in Paris in her 2015 autobiography, Jones writes:

> What took place in these clubs was a kind of choreographed danger, cruising as a form of socializing, contradictory pleasures gathered together in a single place. Energy in the margins that would eventually pour into the mainstream. A whole range of sensations designed to make people happy for one night. These clubs were at their peak a representation of the receptiveness to new ideas that were around at the time; a vivid, breathing and often sweaty symbol of transition.[8]

Jones provides a narrative that might help us think about what business she actually has on the stage of gay rights. The affecting scene described here, one of movement, danger, and desire on the margins—the "whole range of sensations designed to make people happy"—resonates with how she narrates her own career trajectories. Jones experiments with her visual and musical style in the underground spaces of queer sociality, crafting a self for performance that repeatedly flirts with, achieves, and fails at mainstream success. This movement does not define linear life stages as she matures and develops her skills as an artist; rather Jones seems to embrace, and perform in, a space of constant uncertainty, where she is as alluring as she is offensive to mainstream sensibilities.

In 1978, the year Jones performed at the gay rights rally mentioned above, radical activists were critical about the complacency of many homosexuals who seemed happy with the homogenous gay ghettos like the West Village and the Castro, where sociality and pleasure remained tightly localized, while gays and lesbians continued to suffer physical, psychic, and political abuse in the larger world. Keith Haring himself challenged a post-Stonewall status quo when, two years later, he stenciled the words "CLONES GO HOME" on sidewalks and other surfaces, traversing the main routes that connected the East and West Villages of Manhattan. Signed "F.A.F.H.," an acronym for Fags against Facial Hair, this imaginary collective of one aimed its unwelcoming hostility at those gay men who adopted the mustachioed, hypermasculine look pervasive in the bars and on the streets of the gay ghettos (a look not utterly unlike the one worn by bearded hipsters today flooding the West Village's oldest gay bar Julius, pleased with themselves for honoring some imagined history of revolt). The message stenciled in red paint directed these clones away from the East Village for fear that their homogenizing influence would overtake the diversity and uniqueness of his particular downtown scene.[9] If the scene of gay visibility in post-Stonewall New York is one of conflicting desires—the need to assert oneself through non-normative modes of expression versus the desire to publicly perform a hypermasculinity that reproduces the sign of gender privilege, for example—then Jones's channeling of conflicting desires in queer nightlife spaces makes hers the perfect destabilizing body to be at the center of a public scene of pleasure, an outdoor gathering of homosexuals emerging from the margins with different vested interests and sweating through a moment of political transition. It is not complacency and homogeneity that inspires Jones but difference, transition, and the charged transcendent states that are about the merging of bodies in contact and conflict.

The social and political energies that inform queer nightlife spaces translate for Jones directly into a sonic exploration of difference, discordance, and experimentation. It was not necessarily the glamorous theatricality of Studio 54 or the sleekly produced sounds that would cohere as mainstream disco that most inspired Jones's creativity. Describing the first time she sang in public—at the mythic nightlife space the Gallery—Jones writes:

> Clubs were everywhere in New York, out of sight but there for those who knew where they were, and the first time I sang in public, it was Halloween, perfect for me, in New York at the Gallery on West Twenty-Second Street. Twenty-two-year-old Nicky Siano had opened the Gallery in 1972, having consciously designed it as a glowing, throbbing dance palace, and his inventive disc jockeying made it one of the great clubs. His approach to DJing was that of a collagist, cutting up tracks, layering sound effects, suddenly switching the flow, catching you out, lifting you up, weaving a hundred tracks into one so you couldn't hear the join; he was the essence of the idea of the DJ as an improvising composer and dedicated showman. He would say, "When the crowd gets off, I get off," and he wanted to make them scream.[10]

The sound, movement, and DJ-regulated choreographies of places like the Gallery and later the Loft and the Paradise Garage became scenes fundamental to Jones's development as a performer. Her description of sound and the way Siano perceives his aural production as fueling a libidinal build resonate with the formal methods by which Jones's body became manipulated for visual consumption. Collage, cutting up, and layering evoke the very processes by which Jean-Paul Goude graphically designed Jones's public image and created a body of work saturated, to borrow Delany's descriptive terms, with the libidinal energies of cross-racial contact and desire. The fragmentation and sensual exploration across cut-up sonic fields, experienced through an immersion in and contact with a contingent mass of bodies, reflect a field of bodily becoming shaped by and responding to the political energies of a post-Stonewall negotiation between the ecstatic margins and the formation of a coherent, politically viable collective. No scholar has more deftly demonstrated this than music historian Tim Lawrence, whose two volumes on New York City nightlife, spanning from the late 1960s through the 1980s, provide a rich, detailed account of the cultural producers at the heart of the underground spaces inhabited by Jones and Haring.[11] If one is to understand the aural space produced by the DJ as one of multiple lines building, disrupting, and redirecting each other in an energetic, pulsing field, then sonic space—both aural and haptic—animates Jones's body as a field of affective energies. These sensory lines in motion reverberate with those lines that would come to inhabit Jones's flesh when Haring painted her body. The collage and layering of sound anticipate the visually energetic layering of Haring's lines over Jones's flesh. It is here, in the late 1970s prior to meeting Goude and Haring, that one sees how Jones might be perceived as theory made flesh for Haring's lines—animated as they are by histories of bodies in contact and his own experiences in queer underground spaces.

A One-Man Show?

After years working as a model and performing in nightclubs, Grace Jones met the French graphic artist Jean-Paul Goude in 1977. In his first book-length collection of writings and images, the graphic designer and editor discusses his creation of the Grace Jones myth; this is a representational project in which Jones's body arises as an impossible form of black excess and overdetermined primitive fantasy. Goude's photographic and graphic design work received wide attention throughout the 1980s in fashion magazines and commercial advertising. *Jungle Fever*, the 1981 autobiographical work that juxtaposes Goude's meditations on his desire for and fascination with people of color against his graphic layout production, arrives at Grace in its final pages.

In an image Goude refers to as *Nigger Arabesque* , Grace Jones stands on her left leg (figure 3.2). Her two arms outstretched and parallel to the floor, Jones's right leg is lifted off the ground, with knee bent and the bottom of her foot facing up, creating a perpendicular angle against the backdrop of a pale blue wall. As her extended right hand holds a microphone a considerable distance from her face, the other hand reaches back to touch the heel of her upturned foot. The simultaneity of delicate, toned limbs and an extension of bodily form that suggests a movement beyond the contours of the wide-shot frame perfectly emblematizes how Grace Jones circulates as an icon of black beauty in total control of her form and the scene she inhabits. Elegance of posture and a certain kind of black athleticism collide in the frame, generating an iconographic vision that necessarily reverberates with historical representations of blackness and the ways in which primitive fantasy is deeply connected to an aestheticization of bodily form. Goude's articulation of his process in the production of the image and the larger myth of Grace Jones produced Jones as a visual symbol of black excess years before Haring painted her body with neoprimitive writing.

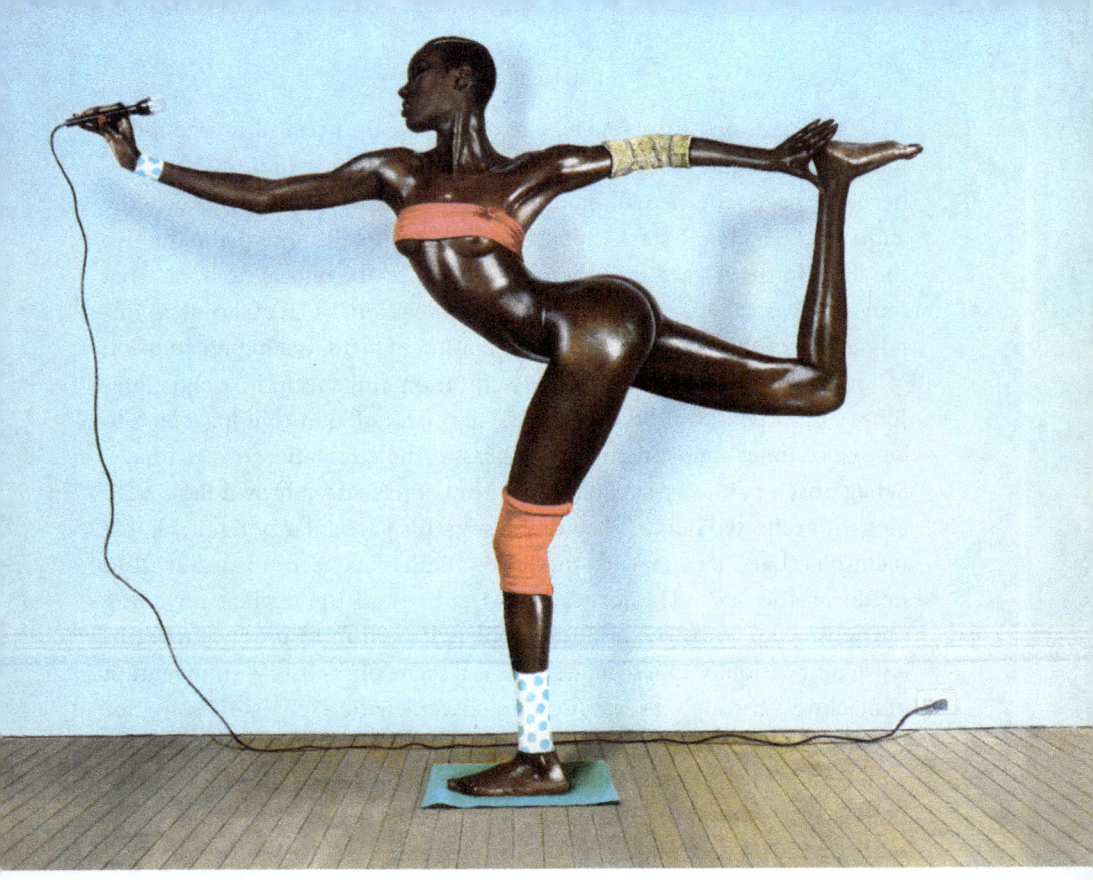

Goude first saw Jones perform at the New York disco Les Mouches. He was taken with the scene in which Jones, in front of gay men, performed her hit single "I Need a Man," dressed in a prom skirt with her torso completely bare. In this moment, Goude sees Jones as something that could animate fashion, a presence that existed beyond mere prettiness, an aesthetic of "shiny" blackness with a face that was "like an African mask." Goude also delights in Jones's masculinity. Commenting on the irony of a woman who looks like a man singing about needing a man in front of a crowd of gay men, he asserts, "No wonder the fruit bars love her!" For Goude, the ultimate force of Jones's image is that it "swings constantly from the near grotesque—from the organ grinder's monkey—to the great African beauty."[12] The arabesque image according to Goude, embodies this aesthetic movement.

Figure 3.2. Jean-Paul Goude, *Nigger Arabesque*, New York, 1978. From Goude, *Jungle Fever*.

In the creation of the image, Goude details a process of incision, dismemberment, and reconnection of Jones's black body (figure 3.3). "I cut her legs apart, lengthened them, turned her body completely to face the audience. . . . Then I started painting, joining up all those pieces to give the illusion that Grace Jones actually posed for the photograph and that only she was capable of assuming such a position." The anatomical impossibility of this pose, Goude's imagination of form, is a hyperextension of Jones's body. Playing with color saturation and sheen, he exaggerates Jones's blackness to produce the rich darkness of skin that has come to be one of Jones's most defining features in the circulation of her image. Set against a painted pastel blue backdrop, Jones's deep brown flesh radiates with reflected light. When discussing this particular portrait, Goude mentions that a dancer with the Joffrey Ballet has been unsuccessful in imitating the pose. The form's impossibility and the explicit unveiling of the process with which he manipulated the film to produce a seamless iconic vision of Jones suggest this is a scene of capture—an invention of blackness through a sexually charged, fetishistic exchange. Posing for Goude, Jones makes her body available for a rewriting of flesh imbued with Goude's fascination with dark-skinned women and the erotic potentials he sees in their bodily characteristics. Goude claims that the "natural flatness" of black dancers' feet inspires him. Unlike the "desperately pointed" feet of white dancers, the flatness of Jones's flexed foot makes the arabesque more interesting to him. It represents a primitive movement that, in his balletic remapping of Jones, registers a "lucky" characteristic of black Americans in their existence at the "intersection of primitive African culture and the civilized west . . . they can pick from both cultures and call it their own."[13]

As the cover art for Jones's 1985 album *Island Life*, Goude's image of Jones's black body resonates with her Caribbean roots. Perched on a deep turquoise square against a sky-blue backdrop, Jones inhabits a color scheme suggestive of a touristic fantasy. Goude creates an aesthetic reduction of signs that evoke a larger history of blackness and Jones's embodiment of island form. This indoor scene of posture, when read against another one of Goude's productions, exhibits the connection between Goude's understanding of Grace's origins and the erotic underpinnings of his aesthetic draw toward her blackness. In an image he titled *Grace at Seven, Imagined*, Goude produced a scene in which a girl representing Jones as a child stands on the porch of a small house in Spanishtown, Jamaica. The young Grace, framed by two white wooden support beams

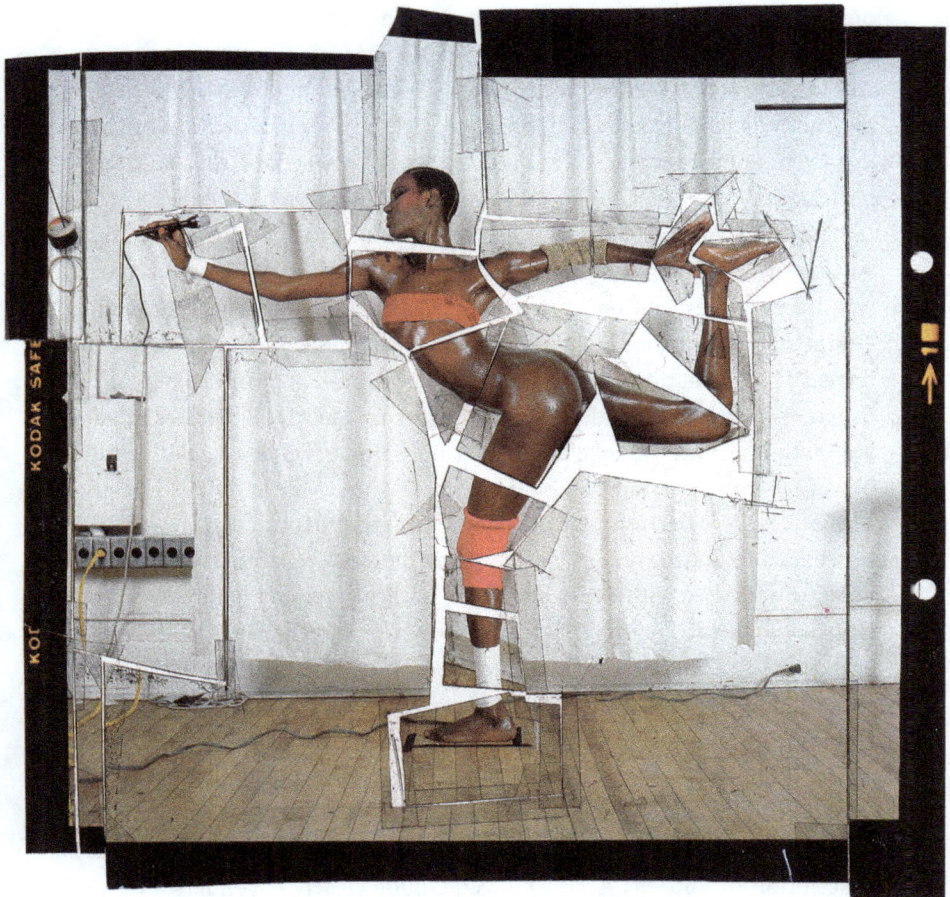

stares straight ahead with her red dress lifted, exposing her naked lower body. The sky above the white dilapidated house is deep blue, and palm trees rise in the background. Goude claims to "show her as the natural exhibitionist she probably was."[14]

Goude's imagination of Jones at age seven—and the hyperbolic control over her image it suggests—represents Goude's return to photographic design after extensive stage work on which they had collaborated. He describes in detail the grand and elaborate spectacles that became part of Jones's mythology as unabashed performer. In one of the shows, a caged tiger is rolled onto the stage. Grace, dressed in a tiger suit, opens the door

Figure 3.3. Jean-Paul Goude, *Untitled*. From Goude, *Jungle Fever*.

of the cage as the lights go out. In the darkness, the sound of roaring tigers fills the space. When the lights go up, Grace is revealed as triumphant, singing as she chews on a piece of meat. While having fun with the stage productions, Goude felt a lack of control in the overall direction of these live events and returned to his picture work, where he "was the undisputed boss."[15]

The image of Grace at seven reflects this return to photographic design. As master of his own design, Goude is able to reinvent a fantasy scenario, where a prepubescent Jones exposes herself for an assumed photographer. Goude's pre-Photoshop manipulation of image reflects a performative intersection of direction, photography, and editing. The promise of realism inherent in the retouched photographic form, one that fabricates a truth via meticulous assemblage and touch-up paint, reflects a visual writing out of desirous possibility. Goude, unclear about where Jones's live performances were headed, revisits her roots through a fantastical articulation of desire. In this image, Goude stages a revelation of flesh that reflects what he decides must have been Jones's nature given her later exhibitionistic tendencies. This imagined primary performance of self, with Goude as master/creator, also inserts Goude into a spectatorial relationship to his subject. The production is a kind of realist documentary fantasy, where Goude is present for Jones's youth, and she performs then, as later, as an object of black beauty for Goude's lascivious consumption. Jones in the late seventies and eighties is what she always was from the beginning. Beyond the articulation of aesthetic primitivism, as evidenced in Goude's description of Jones as African mask, Goude clearly engenders a deeper foundational primitivism in relation to his fantasy of her past. In Goude's imagined rendering, Jones's performance of self is articulated as a constant through time.

Goude's multiple projects with people of color evince a connection between desire and document in ways that resonate with the idea of "theory made flesh." Goude's purported creation of the "Grace Jones myth" could also be understood in these terms, precisely as a fleshing out of theory: in this case, Goude's ideas around blackness given corporeal form via the visual manipulation of Grace Jones's image. Jones as she appears in the arabesque pose is a theoretical manifestation of form, a realist fantasy produced in the execution of the retouched photograph. In the structure of this fantasy, the photographic medium continues to exert powerful associations with the real despite the manipulation of what was actually captured by the camera. The realist fantasy also references Grace Jones as fleshed-out possibility for what is real. She surfaces via photographic manipulation and circulation of image as an ultimate figure of blackness. While the performances and imagery produced by Goude are categorized as myth, they also reinforce the idea of blackness as an essential truth. The contradictory impulses condensed in Goude's conception of Jones are perhaps best captured by his claim that "Grace is modern because she is new and yet reflective of what she has been all along. But now even more so. The androgyny of her body, combined with the darkness of her skin and the power of her morphology (the sum of which would be considered by most bizarre if not unattractive), has been stylized and turned around to her advantage."[16] Here Goude articulates one of the most powerful tenets of modernist aesthetics. The features of blackness become opportunities to re-enliven the old toward new ends, but only through the manipulation and representation of the primitive within knowledgeable and tasteful appropriation.

Goude thus vaunts his own vanguardist artistic craft by turning Jones into an emblem of stable meaning. Embedded within his essayistic recollection of his time with Jones is a constant interplay between his discovery of Jones's inherent talent and aesthetic beauty and his crafty creation of Jones as something fabulous for consumption. His discussion of the creation of the arabesque image reverberates with how he details the construction of her physical body for publicity. Goude cuts her hair in typical Marine style and dresses Jones in clothing with exaggerated shoulders, both of which play off her supposedly masculine form to generate, counterintuitively, a strikingly elegant femininity. He encourages her to learn traditional Japanese dance as a means to re-enliven her image and break from the expected "boogying down or whooping and hollering like all the others."[17] Jones emerges as the ultimate form for Goude's brilliance and his proclivity for a modernist aesthetic. The resulting tension between the new and a presumed constant in black form is a condition of white male writing within a discourse of aesthetic appropriation and projection that is always about a certain kind of erotic desire for knowledge. Goude's self-aggrandizing role in the production of the Grace Jones myth demonstrates how these aesthetic assemblages and representations are never separate from the erotics of encounter and violent sexual framings of otherness.

Goude ends his meditation on a particularly hostile note, making a rather troubling denial of his racism. At the beginning of the section detailing their relationship, he refers to Jones as a "party nigger," an epithet he claims she used to describe herself. The term makes an appearance later, in a much altered context. Goude, discussing the myth he says he has produced, writes, "My masterpiece was a vision entirely my own of what was essentially a simple, naïve person, holding back to what she had always been. Trouble. By the time [Jones's 1981 concert] 'One Man Show' reached the U.S., I knew I had lost her. The 'party nigger' had gone back to what she knew best, and I would have to find a new vehicle."[18] As a closing chapter in a book about Goude's erotic fascination with dark-skinned people, the sentiment contained in this quotation—one of arrogance, racism, and disrespect—implies the unfortunate, inevitable fetishistic manipulations that he will continue to perform on other models. A vehicle awaits beyond his relationship with Jones.

Goude goes on to conclude his discussion with the assertion that his conception of blackness "is free of all social connotations" because of his European identity. He argues that Americans, on the other hand, are unable to "dissociate themselves from the social implications of their artistic evaluation of black people." Goude positions himself outside the liberals who are afraid of their racist impulses and the racist conservatives who only see people of color in a toxic light and therefore cannot fully appreciate their artistic potential. He writes, "So I really find myself in a strange situation, because on the one hand liberals are embarrassed by my attitude, while racists ironically misinterpret me as one of them. And the blacks? I'm not sure." While Goude's naïve categorical approach to his position among racists, liberals, and blacks (a category that seems to include neither racists nor liberals) reads as vulgar and outmoded, it does usefully illuminate how this supposedly socially neutral play with form entangles itself in a fantasy of erotic possibility.

In the end, Goude can only turn back to the consolations of his own genius, precisely because Grace Jones's refusal to remain fixed by his mythic significations is too disconcerting. Jones as a subjective agent could only really enter into the discussion via an acknowledgment of Jones that weds social implication to artistic evaluation. Moments in which Jones challenges or exhausts the aesthetic project are deemed by Goude the inevitable result of Jones's inherently flawed character. The primitive erotic molding clay exerts resistant force in her inability to free herself from what she always was. *Jungle Fever* is a literal writing out of cross-racial desire that documents the production of images and performances that are themselves about the written and reinscribed function of brown and black bodies for artistic consumption.

In a book that I have been citing, cheekily titled *I'll Never Write My Memoirs*, Grace Jones offers her own perspective, fleshing out her intimate relationship with Goude some thirty-five years after the fact (her book was published in 2015). While the book explores, through Jones's eyes, the scenes of creative production described in *Jungle Fever*, the narrative surprisingly resists countering Goude's objectifying and racist tone with its own hostilities. Instead, Jones delves into the psychic space of their exchange and lovingly details the kinds of possibilities that arose for the two of them in their work together. Rather than assert herself as a singular entity according to agential terms, Jones is more interested in exploring what their union meant, delineating the racial field of signification through which Goude approached her body and finding an enlivening mobility within that field. "I admired his work so much I would have done anything he asked me," she writes, before describing the period in which they encountered each other:

> We met at a time when we needed someone—someone who could deepen us, who we could change with, who we could become. That was how it was. And each of us was the one the other one wanted. . . . I was, after all, an art groupie. . . . I wasn't interested if there was no vision. There had to be something that kept me interested. He wanted a living person to whom he could apply his ideas, about desire, blackness, primitive cultures, image, control, someone who was prepared to make their body available. He needed a volunteer.[19]

Jones's voluntary and deeply interested condition of availability coincides with what she describes as a joint necessity. Here, Jones and Goude deepen, change, and become something else together. This poetic scene of complicity, one that softens the objectifying encounters described by Goude, retains the reality of Goude's imposition of racialized ideas around blackness, but the way in which Jones underscores the notion of a "we" alongside Goude's particular desires might indicate something about Jones's preparedness for the project.

Prior to meeting Goude, Jones writes, the difficulties of finding modeling work in Paris seemed insurmountable; she describes famed modeling agent Johnny Casablancas telling her that "selling a black model in Paris is like trying to sell them an old car nobody wants to buy."[20] In defiance of Casablancas, Jones hustles and eventually gains popularity in the Parisian market. This is but one indication of Jones's ability to navigate successfully the racist fields in which she sells her image. Her success also leads her to the Japanese fashion designer Issey Miyake, who in 1976 made her the lead model in his Paris Fashion Week runway show. She finds great inspiration in Miyake's vision and what she learns through exposure to Japanese aesthetics. It is Miyake who introduces Jones to the art of kabuki, an art form she appropriates and cites throughout her career as a singer.[21] Jones not only learns how to craft her blackness and generate interest, she also trades on the exotic, turning to the East to enhance her performance practice, as both a model and a stage performer. This developing knowledge aligns itself with Goude's exotic vision and aesthetic appropriations of otherness. Jones herself argues this connection when she describes his work as that which "made very clear what the color of [her] skin was." She thinks of their work as

> a continuation of where Issey Miyake and Eiki Ishioka [a graphic and costume designer who worked with Jones until her passing in 2012] had been . . . working in imaginary places, in cities not yet invented, with clothing not yet dreamed up, for impossible bodies, for a time that was neither daylight nor night. . . . That was where I saw myself always in between on the way to somewhere else. My head in the moment, but parts of myself strewn across centuries and countries. I had always left myself open to movement and change.[22]

Amidst and through the power of the racial logics that write her and write on her, Jones names her body as a scene of permanent deterritorialization, "always in between on the way to somewhere else."

In Flight at the Paradise Garage

Haring, recalling his introduction to Grace Jones in 1984 via Warhol, told his biographer, "Of course, I had seen Grace Jones before, because she was the diva and disco queen of the whole Paradise Garage scene. But I really, really want to paint her body, because she's the embodiment of everything that's both primitive and pop."[23] Like Goude, Haring had encountered Jones in a nightclub, seeing her before she knew who he was. In his statement of desire to paint Jones's body, we can perceive a resonance with what Goude has previously articulated as Jones's modern character. Haring's "primitive and pop" has a clear relation to Goude's "new and yet reflective of what she has been all along"—a line of understanding that surfaces in the circulation of an iconic figure written out through the reiteration of photographic production and performances in circulation.

Haring's understanding of Jones in terms of the juxtaposition of these two aesthetic modes testifies, in some ways, to the success of Goude's Grace Jones myth.

In Haring's statement, the ambition to paint Jones's body is set in subtle opposition to his knowledge of Jones's diva status—as if Haring's desire to work with Jones exists despite an established persona that is well recognized in the club world he inhabits. When Haring arrives at Jones's body, her flesh has been articulated through a series of excessive symbols of blackness. It is through this surplus of codification that Haring approaches her; he understands her as a sign vehicle mobilized by male artists. Jones's flesh begins to literally accumulate fetish signs as Haring marks her for a further mobilization of the neoprimitive, as established by his predecessor, Goude. Haring argues that his drawing style is similar to Eskimo, African, Mayan, and Aboriginal art, and for him, "Grace is all that put together."[24] Here, indeed, Jones is theory made flesh: Haring conceives of his drawing style as akin to a collection of primitive inscriptions, and of Jones as the perfect reflection of this amalgamation. The register is different from Goude's, of course, but the claim that Jones somehow carries and condenses within her this multitudinous primitivism reverberates with Goude's virtual stretching of Jones's body: no less than Goude's arabesque image does Haring's sense of Jones demand an impossible body. Both Goude and Haring give voice to an urge to create via the body of Grace Jones, and each engenders a fantasy of otherness through the aesthetic posturing of her body. Both men's aesthetic remappings of Jones's body then enter into a system of image circulation: in the case of Goude, as we have seen, via his own dissemination of the work and through Jones's album covers, and in the case of Haring, via the work of photographers like Tseng Kwong Chi and Robert Mapplethorpe (who both documented Jones wearing Haring's paint).

Jones reports in her memoirs that she felt a connection to Haring; in addition to her deep respect for him as an artist, she found something powerful in the way his line operated on her skin (figure 3.4). She is explicit in making the connection between Haring's body art and Goude's manipulations. "What Jean-Paul would do to me in a photograph, externalizing my spirit, Keith did to my actual skin and body," she claims. "They both understood that the truly beautiful is always bizarre. . . . Covered with Haring—his light and joy, his swoops and strokes, his handwriting—I would be dressed perfectly. As he painted me, I could feel myself change."[25] According to Haring, the two left the photo shoot with Mapplethorpe to attend

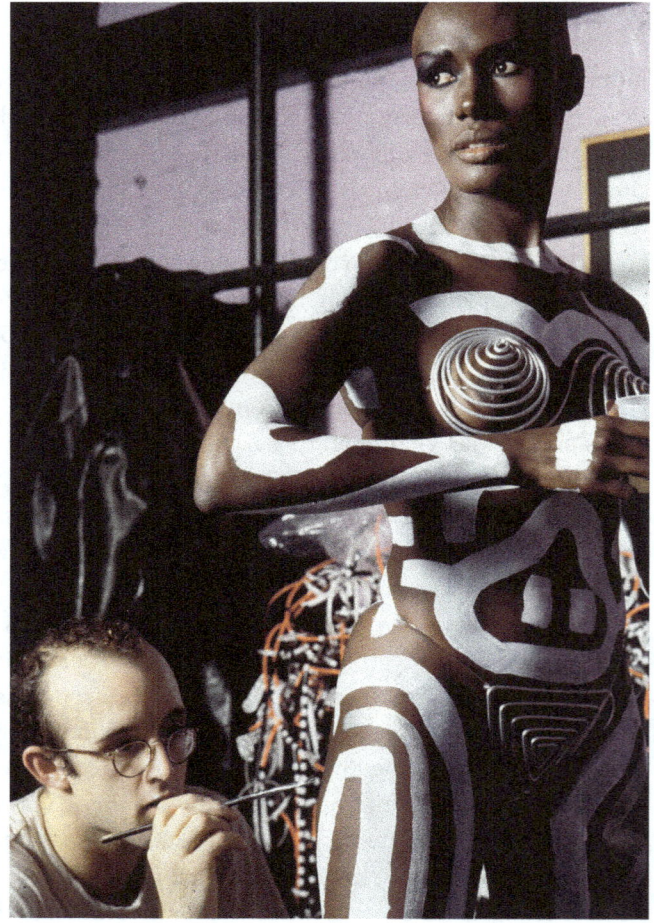

a birthday party, Jones naked and still covered in his line—an anecdote that suggests that Jones did in fact feel perfectly dressed while "covered with Haring."[26] In terms reminiscent of Bill T. Jones's account (discussed in this book's introduction), Grace Jones describes a scene of becoming, a feeling of undergoing a change, that occurred through the process of taking on the line—although here, less a becoming bushman and something more like a bodily openness to sheer change, "always in between on the way to somewhere else."

Figure 3.4. Keith Haring painting Grace Jones at Paradise Garage, New York City, 1985. Photo by Tseng Kwong Chi © Muna Tseng Dance Projects, Inc., www.tsengkwongchi.com. Art by Keith Haring © The Keith Haring Foundation.

The mobility of Haring's line as a vehicle that inspires change, movement, and a provocation of the spirit takes on a particular valence when introduced to the venue of the Paradise Garage—the dance club that was instrumental to both artists' development. For Haring, the Garage was a transformative space of cross-racial contact distinct from the other gay clubs in the city. Moving to the beat of master DJ Larry Levan, Haring and Juan Dubose attended the club regularly for five years. "It's packed," Haring told John Gruen, "and maybe 70 percent of the kids are black, 20 percent are Spanish, and 10 percent are Oriental and white . . . on gay nights [Saturdays] it's nothing like other gay discos, because the kids here are gay but they're really tough street kids—and they're incredibly, incredibly, beautiful! . . . The whole experience was very communal, very spiritual."[27] The scene at the Garage reminded Haring of his hippie days prior to moving to New York, and he likened this communal energy to a Grateful Dead concert. The collective energies of the 1960s bled over into this urban setting, where perhaps the promise of civil rights movements and sexual liberation could be felt as differently marginalized bodies came together, unwashed hippies replaced by hot trade.

For Jones, the Paradise Garage represented a venue where she accessed an exploration in music and performance absent elsewhere in New York City. The disco scene that had been instrumental to her early success and that had shaped her first album had become, like disco music itself, more superficial and commercialized—driven by the performance of hyperconsumption that marked so much of 1980s music and fashion. Both Haring and Jones shuttled between midtown's Studio 54 (the archetypal space of glamorous excess) and the Garage, occupying coveted positions in their ability to gain entrance to both venues. Jones writes, "Studio 54 appealed to my sense of outrage; the underground clubs appealed to my sense of adventure. It was the two sides of me—or two of the many sides—craving freedom. . . . The key was learning how to balance these two sides—the irreverent me who'd turn up at a nightclub like I was the circus coming to town, and the me who was always interested in innovation."[28] Like Haring, Jones describes the Garage as a space of transcendence, with the elevated and tightly secured DJ booth acting as an altar from which the spiritual guide moved his worshiping subjects: "a writhing, dedicated sea of people blissed out on beat, it was the only place where you could get away for a while."[29]

Robert Farris Thompson, in a 1990 memorial essay about Haring, "Requiem for the Degas of the B-Boys," described Jones as one of the "informing spirits" for the artist's work. Thompson celebrates the amalgamation of signs and influences that come together in Haring's production as an opening of Western art to the energies of the nonwhite world: "Adieu Euro-American insularity, hello world beat. . . . Thus came East Africa to Soho." Thompson's piece recalls the occasion on which he was invited to photograph Haring painting Jones at the Paradise Garage; the essay thus places Thompson at the scene of contact. In his account of that event, Thompson coins the descriptive terms that I have taken for this chapter's title: "If, as [Haring] argued, he owed some of his most expressive dancing outlines to close observation of African-Americans performing [at the Garage], then Grace Jones was the ultimate body, the theory most made flesh."[30] Thompson's description of Jones evokes a movement between theory and bodily form. But a curious slippage occurs between the idea of Grace Jones as an ideal canvas for Haring's neoprimitive lines and her ability to make theory flesh. Jones, within the discursive framing offered by Thompson, represents a vehicle for his projected ideas about Haring's Afro-Atlantic sign production. Evocative as Thompson's terms are, it is part of my argument that this claim is another moment of writing on Jones's body, one that depends on an aestheticization of blackness like that practiced by all the artists in this chapter.

The conceptual sequencing of Thompson's account is complex, and contradictory: on the one hand, Jones's flesh becomes theory only in the moment of contact with Haring's lines; on the other hand, that "theory"— as represented by Haring's dancing outline forms—was inspired by his spectatorial relationship to African Americans dancing at the Garage. Are Haring's lines then an overwriting of theory onto the flesh that produced this theory? Or is Jones's flesh situated as a manifestation of a theory that exists prior to its bodily counterpart? The curiously recursive status of Jones's body here—an embodiment of a theory that itself was inspired by the black body—suggests that just as Jones is indeed the perfect person for Haring to paint, she is also the perfect vehicle for the validation of art-historical reading. Grace Jones may act as Haring's theory made flesh, but within Thompson's framework she also acts an indexical referent to ground Thompson's aesthetic theory in a black body: we are again confronted with how white male authorship grounds itself in a physicality mobilized for the production of truth. But what emerges most forcefully from this scene is the excessiveness of Jones's body to these theorizations, and to these reductions of her body to the ground of theory. To keep up with this Jones involves a continual attempt at rewriting the possibilities for her flesh.

Thompson returns to Haring and his dancing forms in a catalog essay for the Whitney Museum's 1997 retrospective. As in the previous essay, Thompson references Degas as a lens to understand Haring's relationship to dancers and the ways a life imbued with dance came to inform his artistic production. Thompson argues that Haring is similar to Degas in his ability to create forms that evinced movement from the streets and clubs of his life. He states that Degas "counterpoised, as equal weights of inspiration, the ballerina and the naked woman. Degas put women in the dance where he could dream about them, in an elegant mixture of document and desire." By contrast, Haring painted "a tougher world, the choreographed braggadocio of black and Puerto Rican New York City men."[31] Thompson's reference to Degas is an art-historical attempt to map a legacy for Haring through the connection to dance, and his understanding of the logic of Degas's work is suggestive in ways Thompson does not fully pursue: if the dance is a way for Degas to transpose the naked female object of desire into elegant dream form, what does this suggest in Haring's documentation of the supposedly brash, macho men of color he encounters on the streets of New York?

Where Degas is said to produce a mixture of document and desire, in the case of Haring, Thompson sticks to document: he reviews the developments of hip-hop musical and dance forms, relating them to historical movements in black Atlantic aesthetics—tracing, for example, how Haring's figures capture the movements of Brazilian capoeira and voguing. Through a discourse of ecstatic inspiration, Thompson energetically riffs on Haring's kinetic forms and the references they elicit. But the line of desire that Thompson claims complements documentation in Degas is never engaged with the same force in his discussion of Haring. If Haring's outline forms and dancing sculptures evince a theory, that theoretical manifestation must be understood in terms not just of its documentary relation to black dance forms but to the desire that structures Haring's perception of them. The citation of dance movement is necessarily connected to a spectatorship of and desire for the very bodies engaged in the movement. Spaces of intense liberation such as the Paradise Garage do not summon spirituality by some inherent connection to ecstatic African dance and its migration to the United States. Rather, they call to bodily possibility precisely in their relation to sexual energy and the erotics of contact.

Gauging that possibility requires a critical vocabulary that attends to the ways in which blackness for Haring as for Jones works as an extravagant signifier, a performative excess that will exceed any documentary trail. In an original and astute analysis of Jones's 2008 video for her song "Corporate Cannibal," Uri McMillan looks at how the performer's body is manipulated in the video, distortions in form that render "a surface-oriented notion of embodiment that embraces liquidity and plural selves, while refusing to reveal Jones' inner psychic depths." Situating the video within the context of her career and thinking through Jones's repeated use of the notion of "surface energy" to describe her work, McMillan forwards a mode of engaging Jones as surface, sensing her through "the synthetic, the stylized, and the superficial, rather than the reliably organic and 'authentic.'"[32] This thinking through surface provides a counterpoint to Thompson: McMillan's reading of surface energy does not attempt to make sense of Jones's presentation through the art-historical stabilization of meaning via visual affinities but instead focuses on the continually morphing and living surface that is Grace Jones in circulation. This approach more readily captures what Jones herself continues to articulate throughout her memoir: the inspiring moments of artistic complicity within exoticist racial frameworks actually suspend her black skin between the various significations we might want to assign to it, even as it disrupts the fantasies of knowing what spaces her body derives from and references (Spanishtown, "Africa," the Caribbean). The image of her body invokes an elsewhere that is always emergent and an assemblage of geographies and historical periods.

In calling attention to the fantasies projected and enacted through Grace Jones's image, I am outlining a structure of artistic engagement in which white male artists like Goude and Haring produce an impossible figure. As written out by these artists, the impossible Grace Jones emerges as a scripted projection of desire that also registers a resistance: these artists are ultimately unable to capture and control Jones's bodily form. While their ideas about what Jones's body represents shapes iconic image and performance production, those very projections fail to keep up with all that Jones's body is able to signify and perform. The impulse to script Jones's body can be understood as an impulse to contain, via artistic authorship, Jones's excessive blackness. And yet in these recordings of and on flesh, these artists engender further avenues for Jones's becoming in their continued insistence on her essentially primitive and utterly modern condition.

Jones's own description of her imagistic creation resonates with what Michelle Stephens has recently described as a "skin act": for Stephens, the supposed signifying stability of black flesh is always undermined by how the black body in image and performance is clearly staged for viewing. Through readings of Lacan and C. L. R. James, Stephens reads this projection in anticipation of an audience as an opportunity for the black performer to disrupt the colonial gaze. In other words, the staging of self—what Stephens characterizes as a lure—introduces something extra-textual that highlights an absence of subjectivity: "The subject-as-artist, the artist-as-actor, offers up a glimmer of his or her missing, invisible, absent, bodily subjectivity that the gazing subject both desires and is fearful of seeing."[33] Stephens, like McMillan, allows us to think about the flesh of the black performer through what it animates rather than what it reveals about some kind of true or specifiable subjectivity or essential geographic provenance. What would it mean to approach Jones at the Paradise Garage as theory made flesh within these surface logics?

From within the elevated altar of the DJ booth, an unidentified person videotaped Jones as she took to the stage in 1985 to perform an extended set that began with her single from that year, "Slave to the Rhythm," and then moved to "Feel Up" and "Pull Up to the Bumper" (hit singles from 1981's *Nightclubbing*) before circling back to "Slave to the Rhythm" as the finale. This extended set, captured via the grainy and now obsolete technology of VHS, records Jones inhabiting Haring's line and performing what she describes as an "Egyptian empress as astronaut. Future turned into graffiti, skin into a canvas, Africa into space."[34] I arrive here, in this Afro-futurist scene, to explore the limits of the notion of Jones as theory made flesh: the moment where theory commences is impossible to locate in such a mediated and self-mediated scene.

Through partial illumination, pillars on stage come alive for brief moments, lit up by the pulse of strobe lights and the flashes of cameras capturing the scene. In the quick alternations between darkness and light, Haring's silver lines, which cover the pillars, leave momentary screen burns on the video record. Jones, already on stage during the opening notes of "Slave to the Rhythm," seems to emerge from the painted architecture, the lines on her body seamlessly meshing with those painted on the set. As more of the stage is illuminated, the entirety of her painted body is revealed, adorned with Haring's neoprimitive script. Spiral-shaped accessories designed by David Spada complement Haring's linear designs, and this layering of silver metal against her flesh does indeed evoke the Afro-futurist aesthetic Jones describes above. After the first number, the stage goes dark again as the sound moves into "Feel Up," with a steady drumbeat. When the lights come up again, Jones is straddling a giant drum painted with Haring's lines, atop of which she will spend the entire song. As she beats the drum, the song builds in momentum, and Jones gyrates in synch with the increasing rhythm, riding the neoprimitive instrument with mounting frenzy.

The racialized script encoded in Haring's line fuels this scene of primitive orgiastic excess. But the scene cannot be fully captured or fully explained by that racialized script: theory will not write itself stably onto this flesh. As the set continues, Jones occupies the entire stage, dancing from one side to the other continuously, physically reaching out and touching her audience. Sweat begins to bead through and overtake Haring's line, creating a blur of white paint across Jones's flesh. In this ephemeral, performative dissolution, the temporality of the line—its applied and provisional nature—becomes visible. This is a line written over the flesh of Jones—it suggests on one level the image of a primitive black body reduced to its carnal nature—and yet this staged production, mobilized as it is by Jones for her audience, is completely unstable. Just like the music with its drum beat that gets lost in the synthetic amplifications of the dance club remix performed live, the line announces itself as a synthetic overlay onto flesh that is itself a palimpsest of the fantasies that produce it. A precivilized past and the future in technological sound are revealed as temporal fantasies, as the artifice through which Jones performs her blackness. They are but two registers of meaning that pulse forth in this animation of the neoprimitive, where Jones herself is suspended between significations, a suspension that animates the spiritual field of collectivity, contingently organized as it is by desire and difference.

Against Rigor Mortis

In a diary passage written shortly after Juan Dubose's death, Haring considers Hieronymus Bosch's triptych *The Garden of Earthly Delights*. The painting's visual texture and the depth of its intensity prompts him to wonder about the history of the visual imagination: "The camera," Haring reflects, "has replaced our idea of reality with a tangible frozen-moment of real-time that we now consider reality."[1] It is Valentine's Day, 1989. He and Gil Vazquez, a young Latino with whom he had developed a close platonic relationship, are in a hotel room in Madrid. After a morning workout, a visit to the Prado Museum, and a failed attempt at clubhopping, Haring sits in his room listening to a tape of Dubose's spinning while watching Vazquez exercise. He writes, "I still find it hard to believe that Juan Dubose is really dead. I kept thinking about it, seeing the funeral and remembering. I suppose I'll always remember these things along with all the good stuff I can remember. The one thing he left forever was his spirit through the music. Even in these tapes of other people's music, somehow his presence is there."[2]

In the longer entry, Haring pursues two separate but related threads—and he calls each of them "reality." In the first, Haring bemoans our lost relationship to the visual, noting that we cannot imagine what it was like to exist before photography. In Bosch's triptych, painted around the turn of the fifteenth century, Haring finds "an imagined or highly aestheticized reality" that stands counter to photography's implied facticity. The paintings of the past make no claim to be tangible records of their contemporary moment, a characteristic he attaches to the time of the image's making: "The reason has something to do with the amount of time encapsulated in this stagnant image. (Condensed-time.) Each face is made of many faces. The distortions (anatomical and conceptual) of the bodies and the use of light make these things have their own reality in a way that a photographic image never can." He then predicts with remarkable accuracy the possibilities that digital imaging and software development will bring to image production. But until this future technology arrives, he argues that we "are lost in what we are convinced is 'real.'"[3] The description of painting, in which the faces index a multiplicity of images and the figures on canvas are laden with layers of time, reverberates with how I have been theorizing Haring's line, though I have tried to draw out a sense of that line less as a stagnant image and more as a vibrant visual sign that energetically communicates a sense of historical drama.

Later in the diary entry, Haring configures "reality" as the reminder of his HIV status, which occurs when he takes his AZT and Zovirax every four hours. "The time in between," he says, "seems totally magical."[4] I get the sense that the moment of listening to Dubose's tape as he watches Vazquez exercise is part of that magical in-between time. It is a living in hopefulness bracketed by harsh realities, as his desires and remembrances are provoked from the collected sounds on the tape, a former lover's artifact of skillful construction. Reading about this audio tape necessarily conjures for me another construction—the silkscreen canvas produced by Warhol I discussed in the introduction of this book. The temporal collage represented by that canvas, Haring and Dubose's rewritten and overlapping bodies, produces a formal intervention that complicates the image as a record of their factual existence before Warhol's camera—pushes the camera's documentary pretensions further into the realm of painting as Haring conceives of it in his diary. Warhol announces his hand in the illumination of bodily form, and that which the fetishistic properties of Polaroid rendered immediate are revealed as my own response to the conceptual manipulation of image. Despite its use of photographic technologies and other mechanical processes, the Warhol silkscreen maintains some of the properties Haring ascribes to classic art's aestheticized and manipulated reality. To use Haring's terminology, Warhol's is a "condensed-time" image, one infused with Haring's desire for nonwhiteness and his hope of becoming other through sexual intimacy. The Haring and Dubose silkscreen contains a critique of reality as imagined in the supposedly objective truth of the photograph. Dubose's tape, meanwhile, also produces historical pulsations, as his initial moment of skillful technical manipulation continues to work in a different register in this present from which he has departed: Dubose's spinning condensed aural lines in animating its first audience and now performs that expansiveness as an animation of an intimate past. The intimate presence of the no longer present now floods into the space of my own writing as I contemplate Warhol's canvas and Haring's words.

There are multiple transversals occurring as I move from Dubose's audio construction to Warhol's silkscreen. In all of this past, I find a way to critique the present through an insistence on queer extension via writing— a writing that resists what in the introduction I called heteroheroics and instead indulges in the queer writing practices inspired by Haring (and by extension a larger legacy that includes Warhol, Barthes, Gysin, Genet, and Giorno). In the case of Haring, what these alternative modes of historical imagining allow is a possibility outside the "real" that imposes on desire a stabilizing morality and insists on singular truths for the bodies of queer subjects.

In this present, I mine the archive of Haring's life for an ongoing intimacy with his line. This is not an archive in the sense of a neatly locatable collection of papers housed within an institutional structure. Instead, it is an archive more loosely imagined as an ever-expanding set of materials that conjure the artist in some way. Those familiar with the work of the late José Esteban Muñoz might recognize the orientation to objects and scenes I am performing in these final pages. Muñoz's 1996 introductory essay to a special issue of *Women and Performance: A Journal of Feminist Theory*, titled "Ephemera as Evidence: Introductory Notes to Queer Acts," had a profound effect on me in not only its ability to articulate the performative quality of ephemera but also its insistence that queer life and its residues necessarily resist the formal structures of historical rigor. The themes that appeared in this essay would be fleshed out in 2009's *Cruising Utopia: The Then and There of Queer Futurity*, where Muñoz delved into the work of Ernst Bloch and theorized queerness as that which is always on the horizon. While the work of queer temporality and the potential of queer gestures in that book are clearly in evidence in—haunting, if you will—the theory of the line I have been drawing out across these chapters, Muñoz's initial working through of queer residue allowed me to see the animating capacity of Haring's line and those artifacts that survive him. So, in the spirit of that essay, this last chapter is a performative gesture against what Muñoz referred to there as the "rigor mortis" of scholarship that satisfies itself with the idea of trading in something like objective historical accuracy.[5]

These pages, sparked by Haring's subjective experience of music and art in the wake of Juan Dubose's death, render multiple lines of experience as I feel through the residue of this life that Haring lived. They represent an avowedly subjective journey through several sites in which Haring continues to exist for me: I look at two of Haring's Greenwich village murals (and the uses to which they have been put in the years since they were made); a canvas Haring painted in protest of the murder of a black man that continues to disturb with its own violent racial fetishism; a supposedly religious piece of work that speaks of a paradoxically earthbound transcendence; a contemporary artist's tribute to Haring that picks up and expands on the thrilling historical energy of his line; and a set of snapshots of Haring and Dubose that return us to the erotic animation of their relationship. I have not strung these sites together in chronological order; they are in fact assembled in resistance to the timeline that makes us think we know the meaning of Haring's life, which I have been thinking about now for a period almost as long as that life lasted. These sites speak to the troubling elements of Haring's desiring racial imagination as well as to that imaginations' complexity. This chapter is a record and performance of ambivalence—which is to say, a testimony to the presence, in the strong sense, of Haring's line.

Once upon a Time

Fashion designer Marc Jacobs wore a black dress of his own creation—something all at once polka dotted, lacy, and flowery—for his summer 2016 photo shoot for *Gayletter*, a queer art and fashion magazine whose cover he had been asked to grace. The dress flirted with ugliness but just looked cheap. Perhaps that was the result of fashion photographer Terry Richardson's signature aesthetic, which had been popularized by his work for magazines such as *Vice* and in fashion advertisements for companies like Diesel. Everyone always looks molested in Richardson's light. In the *Gayletter* cover image, a tanned Jacobs, bare legs splayed, sits atop a bright blue ladder. But it was Haring's line—in the form of penises, sperm, and testicles—that drew my eye to the newsstand: these figures, which populate the upper half of the space behind Jacobs, appear to swallow the designer's scruffy head. Who can upstage Haring's mural for the men's bathroom at the New York City LGBT Community Center? "'Shameless.' Our cover star has the word tattooed across his heart," Abi Benitez and Tom Jackson write in their letter from the editors.[6] "He believes it's something we should all aspire to be. We couldn't agree more," they continue, telling readers that "no matter your gender or sexual expression, you're good just the way you are." This does indeed seem the perfect setting to advance this message, even if it does involve a certain blanding out of the piece's celebration of sexual excess: the penis-centric mural of orgiastic release doesn't necessarily scream "all are welcome and celebrated here."

Haring's mural, painted in 1989 to mark the twentieth anniversary of Stonewall, represents one of the most absorbing public works of his career (figure 4.1). The fluid black line, kept vibrant through conservation and paint touch-ups, is in stark relief against the white bricks and walls that surround those who enter. Painted on the upper portion of all four walls, the mural presents its own garden of earthly delights, organized primarily around penises, masculine-presenting bodies, and jets of sperm. Moreover, in a clear reference to Bosch's protosurrealist morphologies, all these forms are constantly becoming each other: penises sprout legs and start to dance, toes sprout phalluses and send out radiating lines of erotic energy, a drop of semen grows arms and legs and spurts off to land exhausted on the back of a figure sucking its own cock. A torso with a USMC tattoo reads as a nod to masculine trade. Anuses and mouths are filled and exposed, split ass-cheeks revealing a rosebud on one of the walls. These are just a few of the elements that Haring's line inscribes onto this place. It is hard to capture in words the overwhelming spectacle of animated forms that dance and gyrate across the bathroom walls. Haring's inscription of the piece's title captures this linguistic failure. That title, "ONCE UPON A TIME," is painted in blocky capital letters followed by six consecutive marks (_ _ _ _ _ _) that hover somewhere between graphic line and semantic sign: it is impossible to know if these marks indicate the excitement of narrative futurity (a

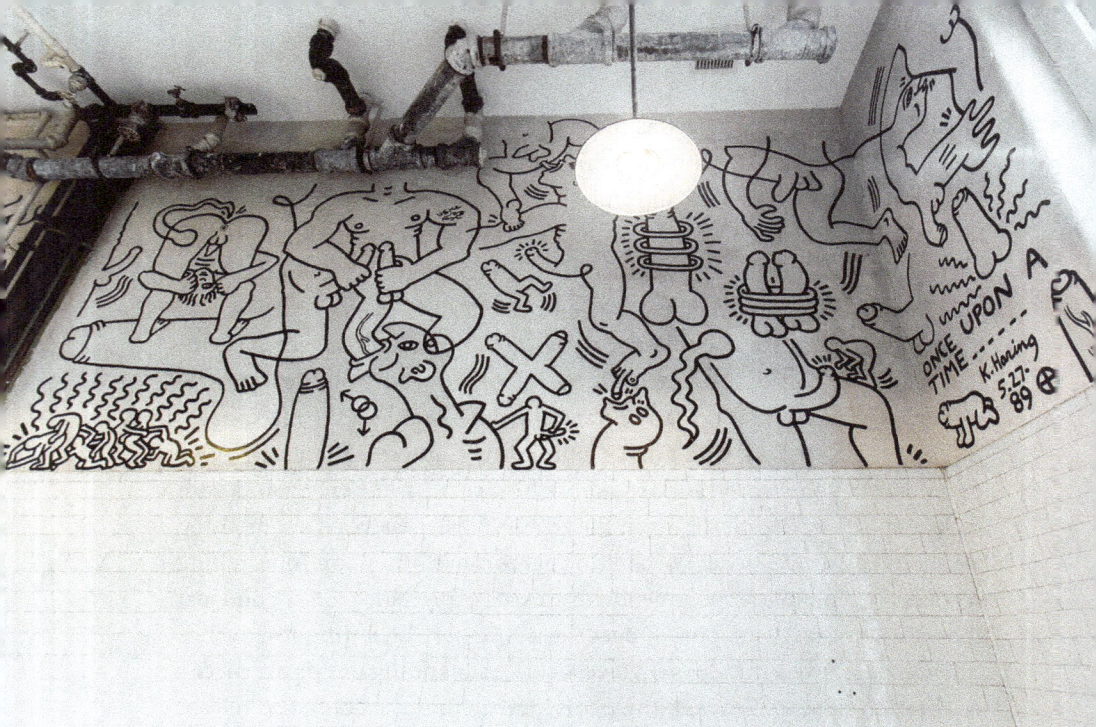

story is about to be told), the nostalgia of narrative past (this is a fairy tale, after all, and it happened in a vanished fantasy realm), or sheer forward movement devoid of semantic meaning.

Missing today are the toilet stalls and urinals, fixtures that were part of the space's original architecture. All that remains are plates and plumbing stubs that suggest what was once there. "WASH YOUR HANDS BEFORE LEAVING THIS ROOM" read the painted words above the space that once held a sink (figure 4.2). For all its excesses and exuberant celebration of carnal acts, that which is absent casts a melancholic glow over this field of longing. Only a few months before his passing, Haring painted an ode to the men's room of his immediate past: the mural evokes the scene of transcendent and sweaty sex that Giorno describes in the memory of meeting Haring discussed in chapter 1. Once upon a time this sexual abandon was possible, suggests the title painted above Haring's signature and the date "5. 27. 89." I have heard from someone who used to work the front desk at

Figure 4.1. Keith Haring, *Once upon a Time*, New York City LGBT Community Center, 1989. Photo by Liz Ligon, 2015. Art by Keith Haring © The Keith Haring Foundation.

the center in the late 1990s that the men's room mural did indeed inspire public sex in the decade following Haring's death. It seems that nobody is getting their hands dirty there today. After major renovations, the Keith Haring Bathroom, as it is currently called, first became a meeting room and now remains open to the public for viewing—and apparently, open for photo shoots. Marc Jacobs claims to have met Haring but to have never known him well. Jacobs survived and has gotten his shameless self together after periods of heroin addiction. The *Gayletter* cover image radiates with historical trauma.

Kids Friendly

A few blocks farther downtown from the center on Carmine Street, one can see another Haring mural. This tamer, cheery aquatic-themed scene featuring figures of swimmers and dolphins appears an appropriate use of

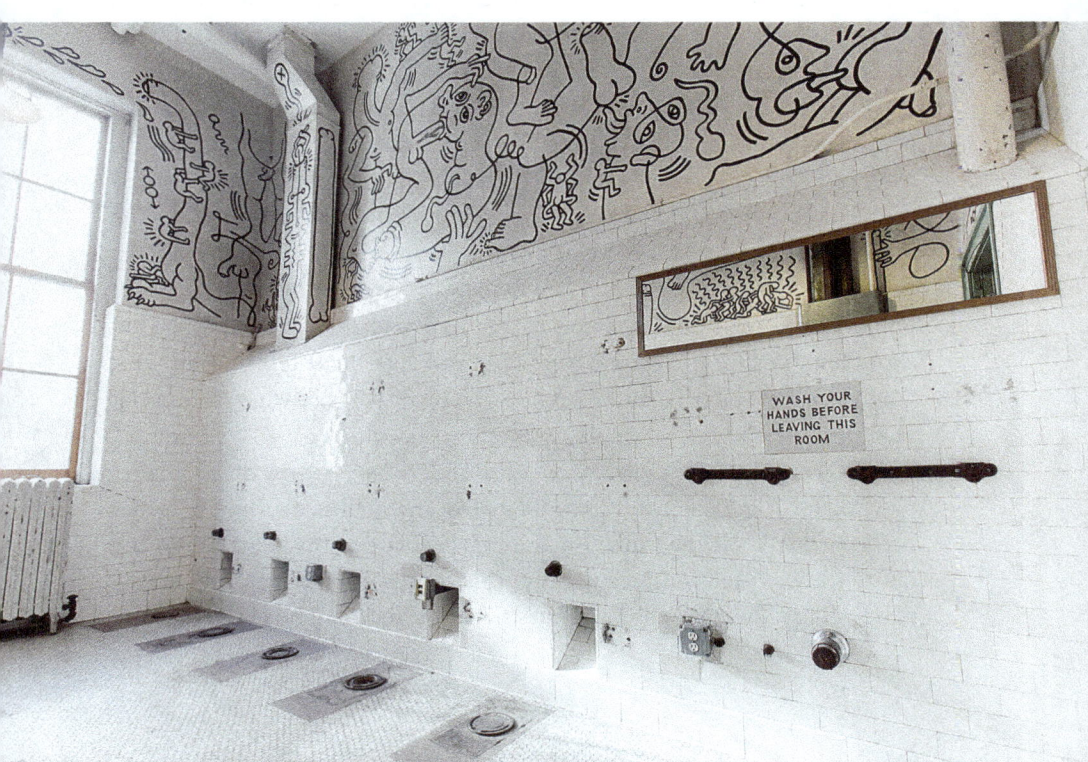

line for the Carmine Street public swimming pool. On a hot summer day, the pool is filled with children.

Filmmaker and photographer Larry Clark, who achieved notoriety with his 1970s book of photographs of drug-taking teens, *Tulsa*, arrived at a new level of national attention as the director of the 1995 film *Kids*. Written by Harmony Korine, the film follows the lives of teenagers in New York City as they have sex, do drugs, and commit crimes, including the violent beating of a man they leave for dead. As day moves into evening, the kids break into the Carmine Street pool after hours and strip down to their underwear. "Damn, your body looks fucking dope," a very white Casper, one of the main characters we have been following throughout the day, says to his female companion. "You think so?" replies the teenage girl in a somewhat flirtatious tone. "I'm serious, yo. It's funny you don't realize how dope a girl's body is until she takes all her clothes off." The camera, which has been moving between Casper and the target of his lascivious admiration, now cuts to focus on a young black man bent over as he removes his pants. Another cut shifts perspective again, as the camera briefly occupies the position of the black youth, who we now understand is looking at the body of the white girl at the center of the conversation. An objectifying gaze from the periphery, this brief moment of looking at young white female flesh suggests what is implicit throughout the film: white urban kids in New York City—shockingly—are in contact with and deeply influenced by a racialized street culture that is both threatening and enabling of their desire within a world of dangerous drug use and sex.

White children behaving badly while immersing themselves in and adopting the culture of "the street"—acting, speaking, and behaving in ways typically associated with black and Latinx urban youth—produces the field through which Korine's story maintains its shock value. The burden of historical representation, the imagined threat a presumably always-oversexed black man poses to the white woman, feeds the register of looking in the film's adoption of the black teenager's gaze. This is but a momentary shift in perspective, as the action then centers on this black youth's performed occupation of the racist script. "That's what I like about summer, a girl's ass . . . mmph. Joy, you ever seen a black man's asshole?" he asks the girl before pulling down his underwear to show off what he is packing (as if in symptomatic avoidance of the dialogue's focus on other body parts). While the camera maintains its focus on his torso during the entire scene, the soundtrack aurally registers his junk through the sound of it hitting either thigh as he gyrates from side to side. The girls laugh and watch this spectacle as you hear one of the other guys say, "Look at it. Look at it." To which one of the girls, speaking off camera, replies, "It's black and beautiful. Look at it." The black youth then asks everyone to be quiet, continuing his proud dance, the sound of flesh hitting flesh more pronounced as the laughter from others subsides momentarily. "That's how I'm gonna be against your ass . . . the sound of me up against your ass. I'm gonna be breakin' that shit, you know what I'm sayin'?" he says before taking a running jump into the swimming pool.

In a 2015 feature on *Kids* that appeared in the style section of the *New York Times* on the occasion of the film's twenty-year anniversary, Ben Detrick reports that the black actor, Harold Hunter, died of a drug-related heart attack at thirty-one years old (coincidentally, the same age Haring was when he passed in 1990). Describing the filming of the pool scene, actor Leo Fitzpatrick, who played the main character Telly, assures Detrick that "those sound effects aren't fake."[7] Knowing that he died young in relative obscurity, I guess we can take comfort in the fact that Hunter actually did have a big dick: even the middle-brow, liberal *New York Times* trades in the basest forms of racist spectacle.

In the pool scene immediately following Hunter's dance, Telly sits poolside with a young girl he hopes to seduce. We have learned at this point in the film that he only has sex with virgins, and we have seen one of these virgins, Jennie (played by Chloë Sevigny), learn that she has become HIV positive after her encounter with Telly—which we have also watched. This threat of HIV transmission thus becomes the central motor of the film's plot, as audiences are invited to enjoy the suspense of watching this white dude player hunt down virgins to deflower and unknowingly infect. "What's that?" the young girl by the pool asks Telly, pointing to a red spot on his chest. "Damn, girl. That's my triple nipple," he answers. Meanwhile, in the water, Hunter's character continues to aggressively pursue Joy, closing in on her and forcing a kiss after she repeatedly rejects his advances.

Through all of this, Keith Haring's child-friendly mural hovers out of focus, the contours of the line losing their definition as a black teenage predator forces himself on a young white girl, and a white virgin-hunter laughs off what the audience understands to be the Kaposi sarcoma lesion that announces the toll the virus has already taken on his young body. Haring feels present but painfully obscured in this film, which documents the ongoing trauma of HIV even as it plays it for cheap thrills. The erotic gaze of the film, one deeply animated by the sexual performance of an aggressive and homophobic masculinity, exaggerates the threat of HIV to raise the stakes of the drama, and Harvey Weinstein distributed its hyped-up, hysterical, after-school-special antics across America through the Disney-owned Miramax with a titillating NC-17 rating.

Woke and (Not) White in the 1980s

According to Harmony Korine, Harold Hunter represented "a lot of the feel and essence" of *Kids*. Exposing himself at the Carmine Street pool, he apparently helped "[break] the ice among the young nervous actors," Detrick reports from his conversation with Leo Fitzpatrick.[8] Rosario Dawson, who also acted in the film, informed Detrick that Hunter told her they were going to get married as they rode the L-train together. What does it mean that this black man, who performed with the grain of black stereotype, can be celebrated for encapsulating the "feel and essence" of an indie film by the white script writer? What was at stake in that performance of endowment among the crew and nervous teenage actors?

In September 1985, Michael Stewart, a twenty-five-year-old African American who also took the L-train, was arrested for writing on a wall with a felt marker at the 1st Avenue subway stop in Manhattan. The ordeal ended at Bellevue Hospital, where Stewart arrived in a coma, his body showing multiple signs of brute force. Thirteen days after the arrest, still at Bellevue, Stewart died. After two grand jury investigations—the first ending in a mistrial—six police officers indicted for perjury and murder were acquitted of all charges. The cases involved a slew of contradictory information from the chief medical examiner, Eliot Gross, who changed his theories on the cause of death throughout both trials. In addition, the defense attorneys successfully exploited inconsistencies in the testimonies of witnesses who claimed to have seen Stewart beaten and choked once he was brought above ground.

Stewart's murder produced a public debate about racial violence and inappropriate force used by police officers; but the justification of his killers' acquittal—which turned on the difficulty of finding consistent evidence that Stewart's beaten body had been perceived by witnesses—points to the systemic inadequacy in these mediated mechanisms of publicity, which are themselves conditioned by racism. The discrepant ways black and white bodies achieve visibility—and the vastly discrepant vulnerability to violence that results—is perhaps nowhere better illustrated than by the book *Art in Transit*, which documented Haring's subway work. Published in 1984, the year before Stewart's murder, the book opens with an image of Haring being arrested for criminal mischief—a television screenshot taken while CBS News did a profile on Haring. The expression on Haring's face hardly appears pained. The image registers more as a staged public-relations move than as cause for distress. In the book's preface, Haring discusses his various encounters with the police. While the arrests range from minor citations to actual handcuffed trips to the station, Haring claims that as they take him to the station, many of the officers praise his work and apologetically let him know they are "just doing their job."[9] Haring, in this moment before Stewart's death, offers little in the way of criticism of the police. He capitalizes on his illegal activity to engender a rebellious mystique. Where Stewart will die in obscurity, an audience seems to be ever present for Haring's daring.

In his journals for 1985, Haring voices outrage at the officers' acquittal and connects it to the impunity white cops enjoy on the rare occasions they are brought to trial for killing black kids. "Continually dismissed, but in their minds, they will never forget. They know they killed him. They will never forget his screams, his face, his blood. . . . I hope in their next life they are tortured like they tortured him." In the same entry, Haring expresses disgust with white men generally and their use of power in the world, and makes the remarkable claim, "I'm sure inside I'm not white."[10] That year, Haring painted *Michael Stewart—USA for Africa*. On this large canvas, over 9.5 feet high and more than 12 feet long, Stewart's naked body extends vertically across almost the entirety of the work, his neck extended to resemble a giraffe's, as a pair of white hands strangles him with what looks like a cord or a piece of metal pipe, his blood-filled eyes bulging and mouth open in horror. Handcuffs circle his wrists: one has the shape of a serpentine beast about to devour the white dove of peace, while a second binds him to a half-seen skeleton. From the right side of the canvas, a huge white leg and foot extend to pin Stewart's foot to the ground. Crosses painted with the same flesh tones as Stewart's tormentors hover in the sky, while a green dollar sign with a hand reaches out to grab Stewart's grotesquely distended neck. In the sky hangs an image of the Earth as if seen from space, red X's marking New York and South Africa. The globe has been cracked open like an egg to release a flow of blood over the foreground. From the sea of blood covering the bottom of the canvas, a multiethnic mass of hands reaches up in drowning despair.

It is, for me, the most difficult piece of Haring's work to look at. I understand the political message, tying the local death of the graffiti artist to apartheid in South Africa in an attempt to render the larger systems of violence at work globally, including capitalism and organized religion, in these connected realms of oppression. But the painting seems to participate in the very forms of exploitation it criticizes, especially by producing an erotic gaze around suffering: Stewart's penis, which sits just below the canvas's dead center and thus organizes the entire composition, is the first thing to draw the spectator's eye. As in most of Haring's work, the figures here are somewhat cartoonish. But even with this distance from realism, the full-frontal image of a naked and strangled black man is too much to bear, resonating as it does with documentary photography of lynching in America—murders justified by the black man's supposedly threatening sexuality. While Michael Stewart enables a critique of white power for Haring, his death—and the production of racialized difference in the case's publicity—also furthers Haring's desire for nonwhiteness. Not only is Haring drawn to the racialized body in subjugation, he desires to incorporate it into his own interiority, and as we know, this desire carries an erotic charge.

A Rusty Line

Uptown at the Cathedral of St. John the Divine, a radiant metallic altarpiece etched with Haring's lines sits in one of the chapels off the main space of worship. Often described as Haring's final work, the triptych takes on a poignancy in its spiritual capacity; it can be seen as Haring's sculpting of his own memorial piece. The Hungarian American interior designer Sam Havadtoy describes how the altarpiece came about in a 1990 introductory statement to a gallery catalog featuring Haring's bronzes. According to Havadtoy, Haring had invited the designer to help decorate his new apartment in 1989. He had plastered over the apartment's brick fireplace; taking Havadtoy's suggestion, Haring carved his lines into the wet plaster and was taken with the medium. The two decided to do an edition of the mantle, using a bronze casting method to create multiples from the inscribed clay. Havadtoy then came up with the idea to use this method for other interior design items such as tables and panels. (Meetings at the Keith Haring Foundation, the offices of which are located in Haring's former studio, often take place today around one such bronze.) Inspired by a miniature altar he had seen in a Geneva gift shop, Havadtoy decided to produce panels in the form of a Russian altar triptych. "Keith arrived. He snapped a tape into the ghetto blaster, turned up the music, sipped a Coke and set to work," recalls Havadtoy, describing the day Haring took a loop knife to clay and inscribed his figures onto the altar panels. He continues:

Keith . . . saw the three altar piece sections. He stared at them and was silent. Then he set to work. He cut into the clay and began to carve freeflowing lines. The images that emerged were unlike the others [that he had carved into the clay panels previous to working on the altar]. They were religious: an interpretation of the life of Christ; a baby held by a pair of hands; hands ascending toward heaven; Christ on the Cross. On one side of the panel he depicted the resurrection. On the other, a fallen angel. When Keith finished, as he stepped back and gazed at his work, he said, "Man, this is really heavy."[11]

Havadtoy then describes Haring's exhausted frailty: "When I'm working I'm fine, but as soon as I stop, it hits me," Haring told Havadtoy immediately after completing the altar. Given that Haring was listening to Juan Dubose's DJ-ing on a cassette tape in Madrid a few months prior as he contemplated Bosch's triptych, I like to imagine that the beats pulled together by his ex-lover were thumping from the ghetto blaster as he worked on the three panels. Perhaps Havadtoy's decision to make altar panels felt like a divine sign to Haring as he recalled the excitement of seeing Bosch's triptych at the Prado. It seems from Haring's final statement ("When I'm working I'm fine") that the production of the altarpiece happened within what he described as that magical in-between time—a space in which the reality of his physical exhaustion, the reminder of his impending death, subsided as his line flowed from his hand.

Havadtoy reads the altar through a typical Christian framework, and while this is a valid interpretation of the imagery, I have always seen something more than Christ, heaven, and hell in the ecstatic scene that traverses the three sections of the triptych. I see a reorientation to what we know about the story of immaculate conception and the potential to be saved or to be damned. A throng of bodies represented by hands in the air spans the bottom of all three panels; bodies come together in a mass that flows across the segments, as if unaware of the vertical lines that divide and cut up the scene before us. Unlike Bosch's triptych, this is not a story told in three distinct worlds, and it does not proceed according to the narrative line of the Dutch master's painting. Haring's is a shimmering field of energetic movement, the torsos with hands raised calling to mind an image of Haring on the dance floor with others on the closing night of the Paradise Garage in 1987. Occupying the highest point of the center panel, a crucifix presses down into the head of a ten-armed figure that cradles a radiant baby at rest. In this figure, Durga, the many-armed Hindu warrior goddess, meets a lactating Virgin Mary: large drops of fluid rain down from this central figure onto the mass of writhing bodies. What are these tear-shaped forms—mother's milk, sweat, blood, semen? All these spiritual fluids evoke pleasure and danger in this scene of transformative movement. Dubose's audio layering digs itself into this scene of Paradise. The work pulses with a beat. On the left side of the central panel, we see that the deity has removed and handed down a halo to the ecstatic mass of dancing bodies; on the flanking panels angels hover, soar, and dip down to be closer to this sweaty crowd, a collective of individuals on the way to somewhere else. The time of the triptych is indeed magic.

A total of nine altars were created from the original clay engravings Haring made. One of these, gifted to the Denver Art Museum by Haring's friend Yoko Ono (figure 4.3), traveled with the *Art AIDS America* show organized by art historian and curator Jonathan David Katz and Tacoma Art Museum's chief curator Rock Hushka. The activist and independent scholar Ted Kerr reported on the controversy surrounding this show when it opened in Tacoma, Washington, in December 2015.[12] Kerr reports that the Tacoma Action Collective staged a die-in to protest the lack of representation of black artists in the show. Between Haring's altarpiece and a work by Jim Hodges—a beautifully delicate tapestry of flowers and leaves composed of silk, cotton, and polyester—the protesters engaged in one of ACT UP's most affecting strategies (a technique the AIDS activist themselves had adopted from antiabortion activists).[13] The bodies of collective members, laid face up on the floor of the museum, figuratively gestured toward those artists of color who have died and the marginalized bodies (those of black trans women, for example) who continue to suffer the effects of HIV disproportionately within a system of neglect that renders them invisible. These dissenting bodies, many of them wearing T-shirts broadcasting the message "stop erasing black people," disrupted the staging of the exhibit, forcing those in attendance to reckon with a glaring absence in the history of AIDS and art. It was the curators' intention, in their historical overview of American AIDS-related art production, to demonstrate how artistic responses to AIDS shaped the future of art through a lasting legacy. Their story, however, reproduced the institutional tendency to privilege the work of white artists over others who have been left out of queer history despite their integral roles. The HIV-positive photographer and dancer Kia Labeija (a former student in a class I taught on Keith Haring) expressed frustration and anger on realizing that she was one of

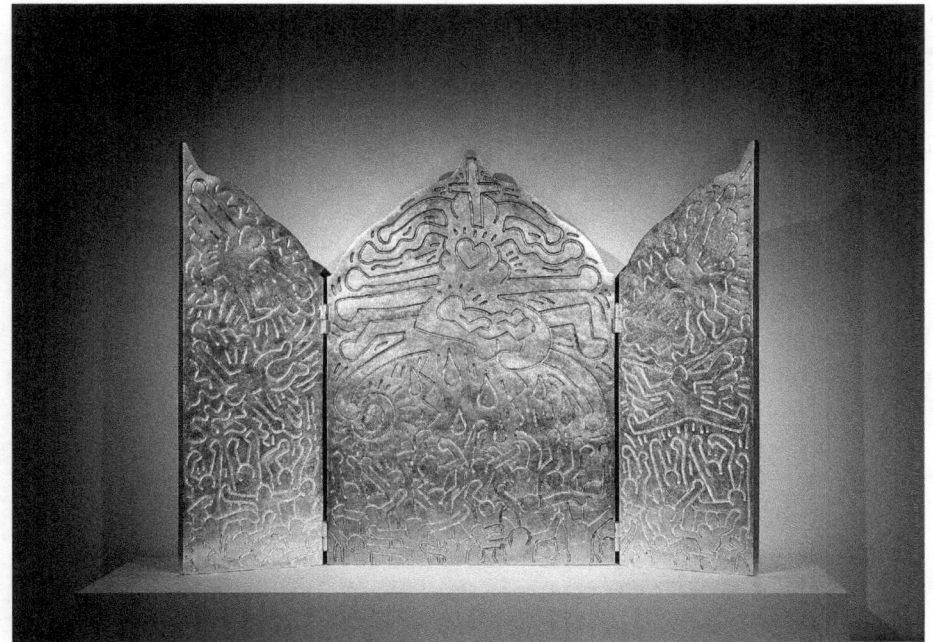

a few black artists in the show. Her tokenized image in a field of whiteness amplified, rather than intervened in, the racist structures of exclusion she hoped to fight.

Amid this controversy, Yoko Ono's gift was reacting in its own way. Unlike the pristinely kept triptych in the Cathedral of St. John the Divine, this traveling altar showed some dinge. When I attended a modified version of the show at the Bronx Museum in the summer 2016, the number of black artists had jumped from five to eight and I noticed something unexpected in Haring's altarpiece. Having spent many hours in silence over the last two decades with the edition in the cathedral, my eye could not help being drawn toward the bottom of the center panel, where it looked as if tea, coffee, or cola had been spilled into the grooves of the dancing figures. I then noticed the reddish-brown hue in other areas of the triptych. The process of oxidation revealed the bronze's assertion of its own life and demonstrated how the material object had traveled and lived, producing

Figure 4.3. Keith Haring, *Altarpiece*, 1990 (cast 1996). White gold patina on bronze, edition 2 of 9. Denver Art Museum: Gift of Yoko Ono, 1996.204A-C. Art by Keith Haring © The Keith Haring Foundation. Photography © Denver Art Museum.

effects in the line that exceeded Haring's hand. Against the tense backdrop of exclusion, the rust seemed to be slowly overtaking and emerging from within the grooves of Haring's bodies. A brownness asserted itself against the silvery gold-leaf patina, refusing a monochromatic expression of spiritual communion in dance.

The Drip: Residual Feelings

In 2014 Joshua Lubin-Levy and I were invited to organize an exhibition for Visual AIDS, a New York City arts organization that supports the work of artists living with HIV and organizes shows related to the continuing history of the epidemic. Taking our title from Muñoz's "Ephemera as Evidence," we imagined the show as an homage to our mentor's pedagogical practice. Students in a class I taught at the New School, Queer Art and the Legacy of AIDS, chose artists, many from the registry maintained by Visual AIDS, and selected works to include in the show. They also wrote essays for the catalog and organized a series of performances that dealt with the role of queer ephemera in the ongoing crisis of AIDS.

One of the pieces we were able to acquire for the show was Rosson Crow's 2010 painting *The Pop Shop* (figure 4.4), which, because of its size (9 × 12 feet), required special effort to transport from a storage unit in New Jersey to the East Village. I spent hours mesmerized by the piece during the run of the show, as it occupied the large wall directly across from the reception desk. In creating the painting, Crow had looked at archival photographs of Keith Haring in the Pop Shop, the commercial venue he had opened in SoHo in 1986 to sell memorabilia featuring his designs.[14] Crow reimagined this store through her signature aesthetic of disorientation, where interiors take on multiple affective energies. While Crow often has a specific location in mind and works from photographic representations of space, her paintings achieve their absorbing effect through a spatial manipulation of interiors, in which objects drip and the boundaries of space blur in what often feels like an LSD-induced vision of interior landscapes. As in a hallucinogenic trip, one is not only subject to variables in the field of vision in Crow's work; one must often also contend with a heightened sensitivity to feelings, where all that one projects onto and in response to the world fuels the adventure with all its potential for pleasure, fear, and revelation. In her undoing of photographic realism through the sculpting of geographies in paint, Crow breaks the indexical relationship between archival images and the reality they purportedly represent to flood scenes

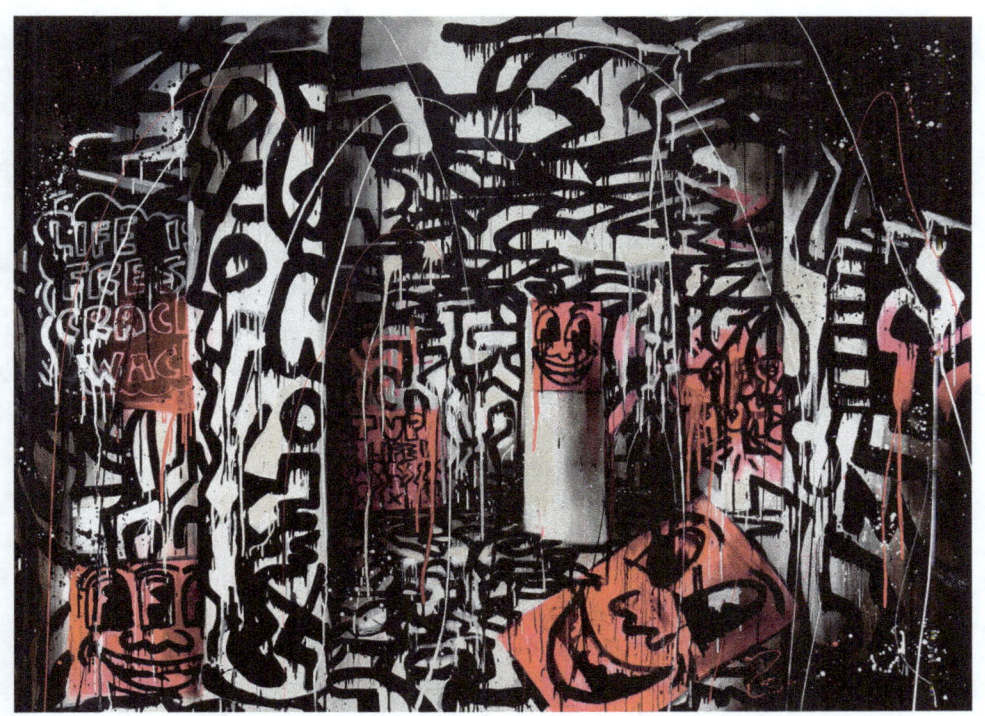

with an extravagant subjective capacity. The scale of the painting often amplifies this effect in its ability to take in and swallow the viewer. Depth of field in Crow's paintings does not just evoke the three-dimensionality of the world but creates a vortex of historical matter and feeling.

Originally shown in 2010 at Jeffrey Deitch's SoHo gallery, Deitch Projects, *The Pop Shop* was part of a larger show entitled *Bowery Boys*, in which Crow explored the history of downtown New York through a focus on spaces that evoked and borrowed from a legacy of "bad boy" aesthetics. Crow researched these space's pasts, trying to get a sense of what downtown New York represented across distinct historical periods. Even when depicting existing cultural spaces, she layered into these works a representation of the past, accentuating what had been demolished or paved over in the constant remaking of the city according to capitalist logic. In Kathy Grayson's essay for the show's catalog, she notes that Crow's "the-

Figure 4.4. Rosson Crow, *The Pop Shop*, 2010. Oil, acrylic, and enamel on canvas, 108 × 144 inches. © Rosson Crow.

atrical confabulations collapse centuries and synthesize styles to reveal the multiply haunted nature of interior space and the affinities that align across time."[15] To enter Crow's version of the Pop Shop does indeed require allowing oneself to be absorbed into a haunted scene. In the photographs Crow references, Haring poses in his shiny new store, where every surface is dramatically painted with his line (the walls and columns in the SoHo shop were all white, the lines black). In Haring's energetic line work in the Pop Shop, the large scale of the drawings on the pillars contrasts with the more compressed figures on the walls, producing a dizzying effect that Crow's manipulations pick up on and accentuate. In the pages of Crow's sketchbook, one sees how she redraws different parts of the photographs, placing spatial elements at disorienting angles, repeating them, and overlapping them.[16] She cuts up space and collages it, producing an uncanny landscape that retains elements of the original photograph but looks completely distinct. Adding to the sense of disorientation, Crow then layers into the space several versions of a square smiling face Haring once drew, and reproduces a portion of the *Crack Is Wack* mural Haring painted in 1986 at a handball court at 2nd Avenue and 128th Street. "ACT UP, Fight AIDS!" is scribbled to the side of the image, indicating text that she might incorporate into the final painting. As the sketch comes to canvas, the contours of the cited material blur in a field of gestural movement: what had been collage becomes a surreally contoured interior space. The material is visually indexed, but Crow's theatrical rendering of her sketch onto canvas obscures the process of collage, as the signifiers of the past seem to hover in space, in a funhouse-mirror version of the Pop Shop.

The affective work of Crow's painting lies not just in its distortion of space but also in the physics of her painterly gesture. If Haring's line might be understood as one that animates and draws from the kinetic energy of dance, what does it mean when Crow cites that line and repaints it in such a way that drips—disruptions to the clean directionality of the line—become exaggerated? One of Crow's signature gestures is to produce drips and splatters all over her canvases. She dramatizes the opposing forces of velocity and gravity in these moves, complementing the heavy drip of paint with Pollack-like arcs and splatters. Objects and entire environments are thus produced in all their visual clarity, even as they appear to be drooping or melting, as if the scene we have come upon is about to lose its recognizable contours.

Crow's poetic and formally structured messiness conveys something crucial about the process of being with history, and about the attempt to sense the past through the inhabitation of interiors pregnant with what feels like a kind of temporal energy. Hers are canvases in which it is difficult to say whether these environments and all they contain are in the process of becoming residue or whether these spaces and their objects are instead emerging from some heap of undifferentiated matter. This is a truly new way of dramatizing suspension between places and eras—making historical movement visible and perceptible through the velocities of the brush and the slow drip of paint. Crow's painting, with its color palette of hot pink, black, and dingy white, evokes a complicated field of emotions. On the one hand, *The Pop Shop* undoes the general cheeriness of Haring's commercial project and its utopic dream of making art available to everyone. And at the same time, Crow's work picks up on a gravity to Haring's line, one that exceeds the easily consumable imagery we so often associate with him. This is the genius of Crow's color; it draws on the urgencies of AIDS activism and the devastation of crack addiction to mark the complex field of politics and emotion that fed the Pop Shop. The painting performs a queer line, dripping with gravity and reaching into the past. The photographic image is reimagined as a sign with potential in excess of the reality it refers to. The scene of Haring in the Pop Shop becomes subject to the forces of time, its residues and its emergences. The picture offers us historical depth not as concept but as sensation.

These Fucking Beautiful Boys:

At the Beach after Reading *Camera Lucida*

In the introduction to this book, I describe being overcome with emotion at the sight of Juan Dubose and Keith Haring in a set of Polaroids in Andy Warhol's archive. That experience has more recently been reinvigorated by an encounter with another set of photos—these from Tseng Kwong Chi's archive. In 1982, Haring brought Dubose with him to Brazil. There are several photos from this trip. Most of them interest me for the general reason that they involve Haring and Dubose, and because the two look happy under bright sun and vibrant skies. They are young and attractive and clearly very much into each other. Images of them playing in a shallow surf evoke a sensual pleasure, and this vacation-inflected scene allows me to imagine some quality of relaxed intimacy during the early period of their relationship. It seems as if all of Haring's overwrought desire to possess a mass of dark-featured boys has dissipated a bit in these blue waters. This is how I imagine it, anyway.

And yet, one photo—with the boys out of the water and lounging on the sand—feels particularly charged (figure 4.5). Propped on his left arm, Dubose reaches over, it seems, to tweak Haring's nipple. A slight blur in the shape of Haring's head elevated off his towel suggests that his body is reflexively responding, moving in reaction, to this pinch. His ab muscles flex perhaps mid-laugh or in concert with the wince of slight pain. In the foreground lie Haring's glasses, and this object, removed from his face and in danger of being crushed, made me stop and spend time with this image. In fact, I noticed them long before I became aware of the central touch between the two boys; Haring's glasses kept me from immediately seeing the much more obviously exciting tweaking of flesh. In those Warhol Polaroids and silkscreens, and in so many popular images of Haring, his round glasses are a defining feature, as iconic as Warhol's wig. This feature of Haring's costume, set aside as it is here, demands my attention as an animating fetish. This is the thing that pierces, the Barthesian punctum that wounds me, the piece of the image that forces me to a state of intimacy that is more turbulent than a general "research" interest in the artist at the heart of this book (it is, of course, this intimacy that has driven that research interest.)[17] Allowing myself into this opening, I begin to see the formal properties of the image through a projection of sensation, feeling myself on this beach via a kind of haptic fantasy. I think I can guess what the sun and sand might feel like or what Haring might be experiencing as Dubose squeezes a tender nipple between two fingers, suddenly and out of nowhere in a playful and loving gesture. I pull experience from my life to put myself at the scene. I have never been to Brazil. I know this very well, but all the same, I continue to inhabit the frame of contact—between them, and between me and them. Haring has ceded 20/20 vision in setting his glasses aside and turning his head away from the camera, away from me as the viewer of this image, and I take advantage of this vulnerability— never mind that I, like so many others before me, have somehow erased Tseng in this whole scene of looking. But the photograph is a record of Tseng's gesture, too. These fucking beautiful boys drive me crazy.

Tseng reaches out, drawing a line with this photograph into the future. In Vilém Flusser's writing on gesture, the media philosopher, like Barthes, attempts to elaborate a philosophical condition of the photograph that is attentive both to its technological dimension and to its invocation of and call to human subjectivity. For Flusser, all apprehension of the world involves a manipulation. A hand asserts itself, whether in a literal or a metaphorical way, in every instance that a person interprets what she encounters—

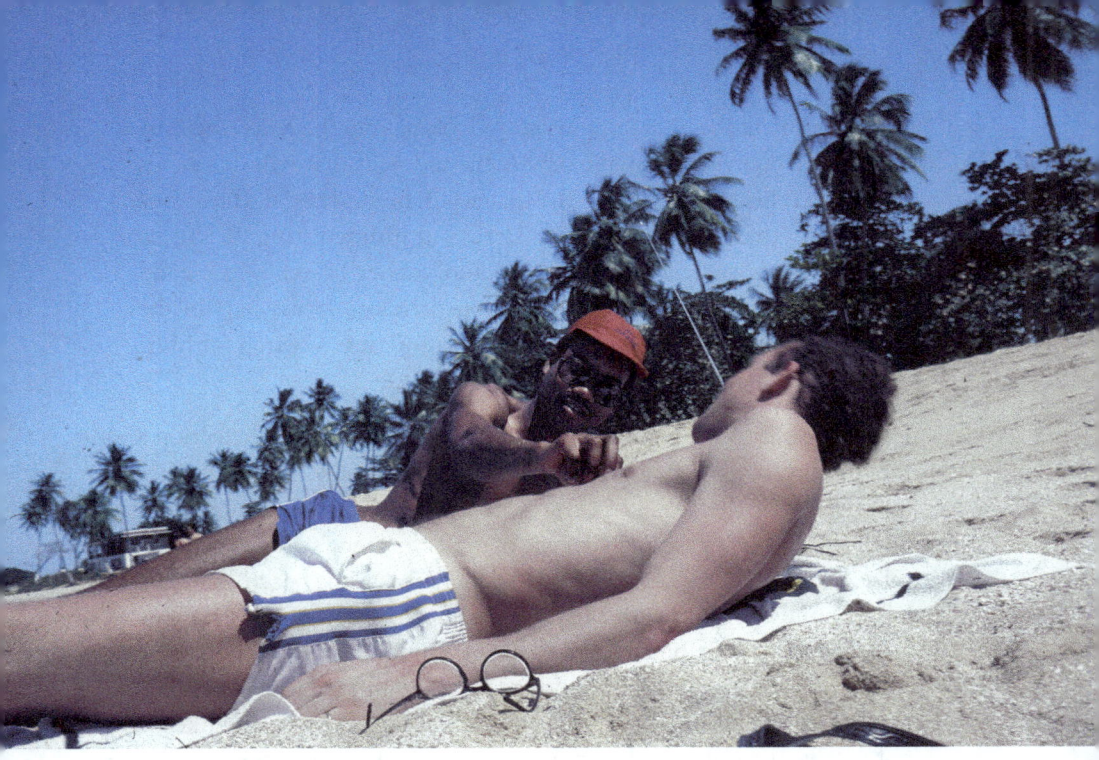

the very act of beholding something is an instance of manipulation; one affects an object in the moment that one is affected by it. The mirror embedded in the single-reflex camera, which internally reflects the world back to the photographer in the act of framing an image, is a device that for Flusser highlights the philosopher in the photographer—that selective agent who "rejects all possible images" in favor of one, and "condemns all the other possible images . . . to the realm of lost virtualities." Photography is a gestural criticism where "choice functions as a projection into the future."[18] This active subject, the photographer, sees herself in the process of image selection, using the device to home in on a moment and then releasing this moment in hopes that it will penetrate others. Hers is not an unobtrusive act of simply capturing what is there but rather represents a vested bracketing of the world that presupposes a reckoning with a future of looks. I am interested here in the way Flusser describes the self-reflexive performance of the photographer as already containing the notion of the photograph's own reception:

Figure 4.5. Juan Dubose (*left*) and Keith Haring on the beach, Brazil, 1982. Photo by Tseng Kwong Chi © Muna Tseng Dance Projects, Inc., www.tsengkwongchi.com.

The moment the photographer stops looking into the reflecting mirror (whether real or imaginary) is the moment that will define his image. If he stops too early, the image will be superficial. If he stops too late, the image will be confused and uninteresting. It will be penetrating and revealing if the photographer has chosen a good moment to stop reflecting. Reflection therefore forms part of the photographer's search and his manipulation. It is a search for himself and a manipulation of himself.[19]

Flusser's description here, shuttling as it does between self-reflection and the anticipatory effects of the photograph on those who will encounter it, aligns with the space of complicity I have explored throughout this book as its own unpredictable scene of making. Tseng's photographic self-reflexivity brings me back to my introduction. On the beach in Brazil, as in the London studio with Bill T. Jones, Tseng is complicit in a scene of cross-racial desires, but the stakes of this complicity feel less heightened here, outside the professional studio. Or rather, this is the impression that penetrates me, knowing that this particular image has not and likely will not receive the same kind of exposure across time. It will not become an image repeatedly inserted into a timeline of Haring's short life as it moves from rapidly mounting fame to rapidly approaching death.

I can have this image, and all of them, here alone at my desk. Those glasses. They are sitting in sand recently softened by a tide that has receded. One lens manages to sit atop Haring's beach towel, and near it, I notice a glimmer. Haring wears a silver ring on his left pinky. Is this an approximation of a wedding band, a sign of commitment that touches up against the designated finger of a state-sanctioned union? (In none of the other photos does Dubose have a complementary ring, refusing immediate confirmation of this speculation.) In another photo, they are standing against a wall of rock, Dubose's arm bent at a ninety-degree angle over Haring's shoulder, his left hand suspended over Haring's chest and casting a shadow against the artist's Pep Boys T-shirt (figure 4.6). (Apparently, Haring owned more than one of these. Was it the round glasses worn by one of these Pep Boys that drew him to the image?) Haring, head cocked in a slight downward gaze, looks as if he is about to kiss Dubose's brown arm. Meanwhile, Dubose seems to be giving Tseng a bit of sass, smiling slightly at the camera with his right hand on his hip. Upon closer inspection, however, the fingers at his midsection reveal themselves as those of Haring, who is holding his lover against a slightly flexed bicep. Dubose's

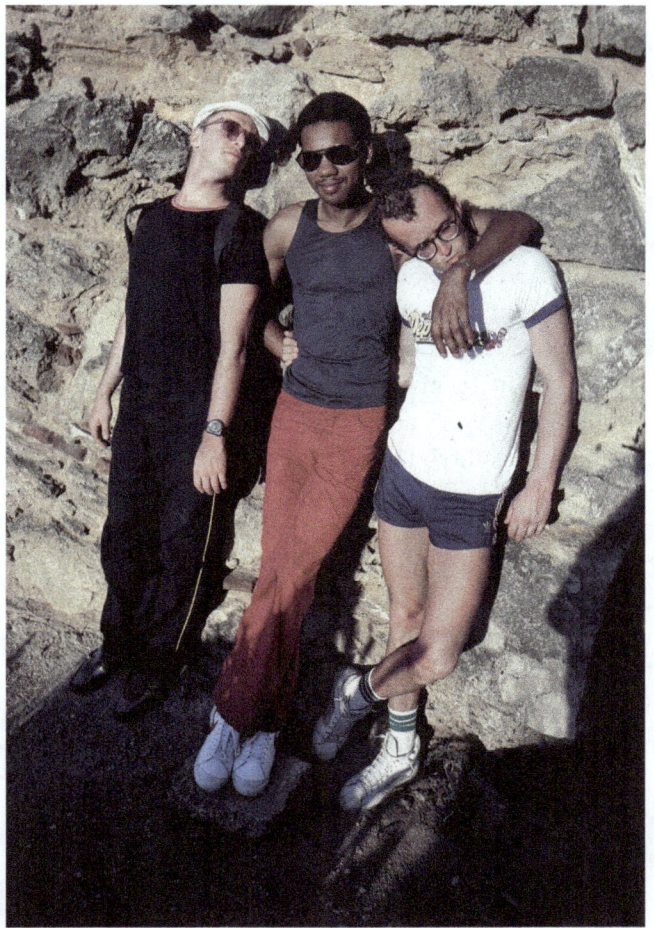

right arm now appears to be serving as buttress against the sharp rocks at his back. I do not know who the white man standing next to them is. Kenny Scharf? This third wheel does not feel relevant—my process of se-lection further revealing itself in my attempt to dig into a space of imag-ined intimacy.

Knowing that my access to the truth of Haring and Dubose's trip is limited, I am suspended between apprehension of these visual documents and their stabilized codification within a rigorously verifiable historical

Figure 4.6. Keith Haring (*right*) with Juan Dubose (*middle*) and unidentified man in Brazil, 1982. Photo by Tseng Kwong Chi © Muna Tseng Dance Projects, Inc., www.tsengkwongchi.com.

narrative. I am reminded of my spectatorial condition as the only verifiable subject of the images, having accepted Barthes's thesis on the Warholian image ("the one who looks in the absence of the one who makes" is the real subject of the work) and extrapolated it to all images.[20] Yet, if Barthes and Flusser seem intent on an inescapable self-reflexive condition inherent to photography, why then would they try to write about such narcissistic reflections and communicate them to others? What can one truly know about the world if all that is experienced is the isolation of the individual against the other's unknowability? These journeys into the past through archival research only seem to amplify this condition, as my demands for a coherent story about Keith Haring and cross-racial desire meet with resistance at every turn. Barthes's fragments and Flusser's philosophical gestures, however, ask that we leave traces of our restricted self-reflexive negotiations with the world. They define our gestures as the animating force of the future. This book has been a trip generated from Haring's painted traces, an attempt to inhabit his line beyond the linear stories that try to locate it in a knowable and definable past.

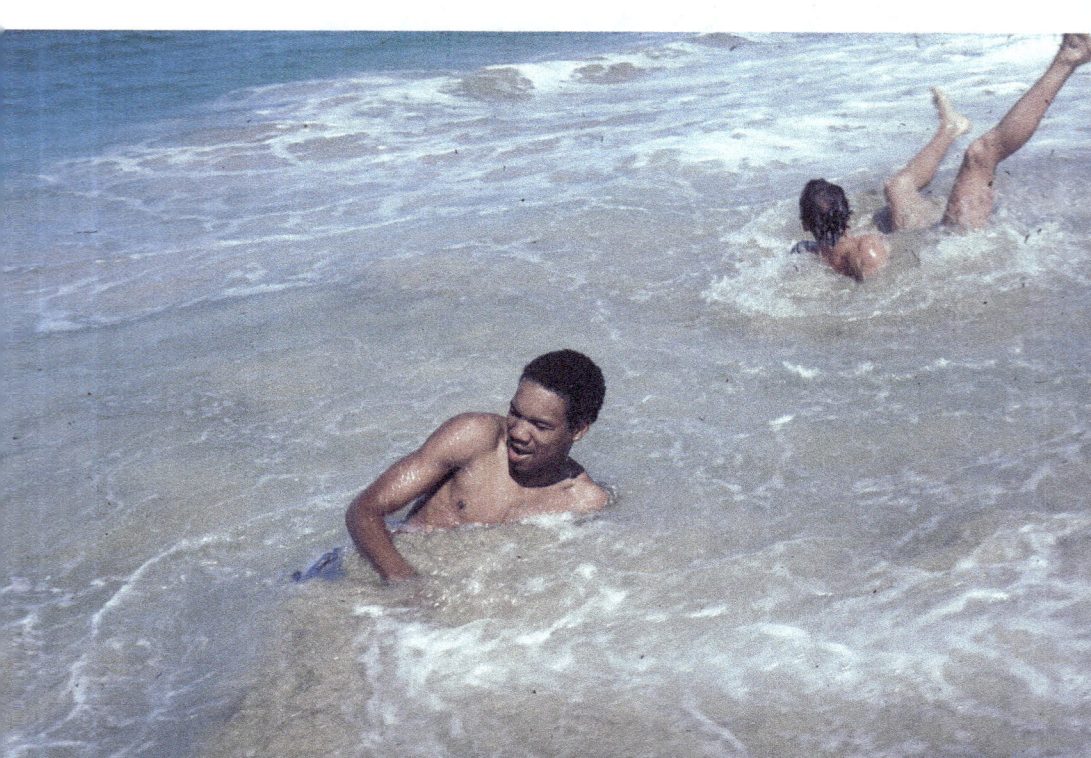

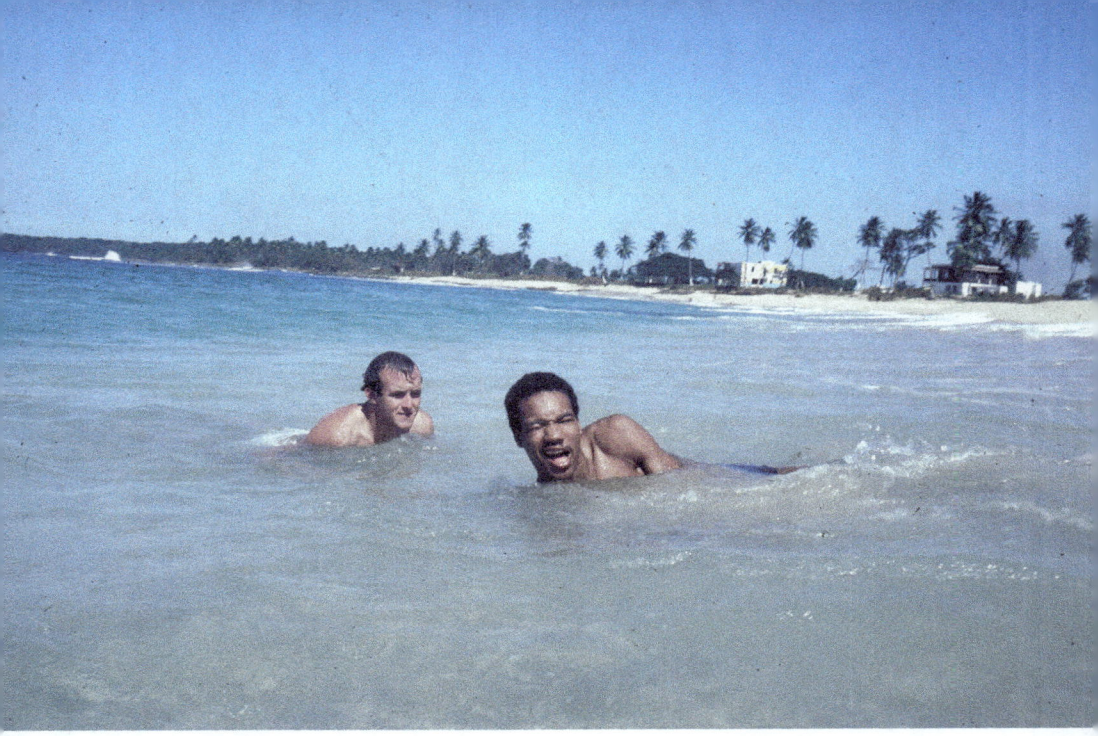

Here, at the end, I leave you with two final images from the 1982 trip to Brazil (figures 4.7 and 4.8). In the first, the boys are partially submerged in clear water that has been colored by the churning of sand. Has a wave just hit, bringing them closer to the shore? It certainly appears that Haring may have lost his footing at some point. Turned away from Tseng's camera, his legs are akimbo and jut out in front of him. Dubose is in the foreground, the water reflecting off his exposed torso. The photograph's moment highlights a distance between them. In a second image, which appears to have been taken a moment later, the water seems to have settled; the sand is no longer churning, and their bodies are more submerged. Haring has recovered himself and faces Dubose. The distance between them has significantly shortened. Haring, his eyes set on his lover, appears to be following a line like a shark closing in on its prey. (It is hard to look at that ocean and not think of the sharks we know it somewhere contains.) For now, we are in the magic in between.

Figure 4.8. Keith Haring and Juan Dubose on the beach in Brazil, 1982. Photo by Tseng Kwong Chi © Muna Tseng Dance Projects, Inc., www.tsengkwongchi.com.

Introduction

1 John Gruen, *Keith Haring*, 96.

2 John Gruen, *Keith Haring*, 95–96.

3 Miller, *Bringing Out Roland Barthes*, 7. Miller's negotiations with the deceased Barthes very much resonate with my feelings around Keith Haring, a queer predecessor who preceded me in his encounter with New York City and whose writing and art enables me to imagine a shared intimacy with him. This intimacy has in turn animated much of what I access as queer potentiality in my experience of the city.

4 Cvetkovich, *Archive of Feelings*, 7.

5 In the last thirty years, various critics and art historians have done the valuable work of exploring Haring's debt to African and other non-Western artistic forms. Among the most notable are van de Guchte, "Chance Favors the Prepared Mind"; Thompson, "Requiem for the Degas of the B-boys"; and Thompson, "Haring and the Dance." This work is indispensable to any account of Haring's development as an artist, and it deeply informs my work in the chapters that follow. Meanwhile, there is a growing bibliography on Haring's relation to his black and Latinx collaborators, friends, acquaintances, and lovers: see, for example, Cruz-Malavé, *Queer Latino Testimonio*; Negrón-Muntaner, *Boricua Pop*; and Woubshet, *Calendar of Loss*. While I have learned much from the first group's tracing of Haring's relations to nonwhite cultures, and while I share the second group's wariness of the fantasies that informed his relations to those cultures, I have resisted taking this work as license to critique Haring as an appropriative artist in order to explore the ambivalence that his work is born of and continues to perform.

6 John Gruen, *Keith Haring* 96.

7 John Gruen, *Keith Haring* 98.

8 Mercer, *Welcome to the Jungle*, 176.

9 This language notwithstanding, Mercer's vision of the way this process oper-
ates in Mapplethorpe is far from stagnant: he goes on to consider how Mapplethorpe "implicate[s] himself in the field of vision by a kind of participatory
observation" and thereby makes his work interpretable as "an elementary starting point of an implicit critique of racism and ethnocentrism in Western aesthetics" (*Welcome to the Jungle*, 195, 196).

10 Marcus, "Uses of Complicity," 100.

11 Marcus, "Uses of Complicity," 101.

12 See Musser, *Sensational Flesh*.

13 John Gruen, *Keith Haring*, 88.

14 John Gruen, *Keith Haring*, 77.

15 John Gruen, *Keith Haring*.

16 John Gruen, *Keith Haring*, 80.

17 John Gruen, *Keith Haring*, 195.

18 Warhol, *Andy Warhol Diaries*, 521.

19 Ricard, "Radiant Child."

20 Cruz-Malavé, *Queer Latino Testimonio*, 8.

21 For a searching treatment of the desire to touch the past, and the queerness of
that desire, see Dinshaw, *Getting Medieval*, 1–54.

22 Doyle, *Hold It against Me*.

23 My thinking here has been deeply influenced by José Esteban Muñoz, who
writes of "queerness's pull" as a "something else that we can feel, that we must
feel" (*Cruising Utopia*, 185).

24 Wall text, *Keith Haring: Retrospective*.

25 Sheff, "Keith Haring."

26 Among the texts that have most shaped my understanding of AIDS/HIV history, publicity, and activism are Patton, *Inventing AIDS*; Crimp, *Melancholia
and Moralism*; and Watney, *Policing Desire*.

27 Boyd, "Reagan Urges Abstinence," A13.

28 Taylor, "You Are Here."

29 See, for example, Browning, *Infectious Rhythm*, on the racialized legacies of
some of this biologized discourse.

30 Recent work on queer temporality has usefully explored the connections between these nonstandard intimacies and nonstandard timelines: as Freeman
writes, "sexually dissident bodies and stigmatized erotic encounters—
themselves powerful reorientations of supposedly natural, physiological
impulses—perform the contest between modernity's standard beat and the
'sudden rise' of possibilities lost to the past or yearning toward the future"
(*Time Binds*, 171).

31 To my knowledge, this silkscreen has been reproduced only in the first edition
of Haring, *Keith Haring Journals*. The silkscreen was omitted from the 2010
edition.

32 Barthes, "That Old Thing, Art," 371. For an extended analysis of seriality and
technique in Warhol's work, see Ganis, *Andy Warhol's Serial Photography*.

1. Desire in Transit

1 Haring, *Keith Haring Journals* (1996), 70.
2 Genet, *Fragments of the Artwork*, 92.
3 Genet, *Fragments of the Artwork*, 101–2.
4 Gysin, "Sculpted Line," 291.
5 Van de Guchte, "Chance Favors the Prepared Mind."
6 Van de Guchte, "Chance Favors the Prepared Mind," 85.
7 Omi and Winant, *Racial Formation in the United States.*
8 Coco Fusco's seminal text "The Other History of Intercultural Performance" documents this larger history of racist exhibition practices vis-à-vis her performance collaboration *Couple in the Cage*, with Guillermo Gómez-Peña. Additionally, Jennifer A. González's more recent work, *Subject to Display*, examines how contemporary artists have negotiated and disrupted the racialized technologies of display inherent to the history of art exhibition.
9 Haring, *Keith Haring Journals* (1996), 128.
10 Haring, *Keith Haring Journals* (1996), 130.
11 Platow, *Keith Haring*, 86.
12 Haring, *Keith Haring Journals* (1996), 45–48.
13 Giorno, *You Got to Burn*, 66.
14 Giorno, *You Got to Burn*, 67.
15 Giorno, *You Got to Burn*, 68.
16 Giorno, *You Got to Burn*, 69.
17 Giorno, *You Got to Burn*, 70–71.
18 Giorno, *You Got to Burn*, 68–69.
19 Giorno, *You Got to Burn*, 73.
20 Giorno, *You Got to Burn*, 74.
21 For an excellent discussion of Haring's political evolution in relation to aesthetic traditions in counterculture, see Roth, "From Irony to the Apocalypse."
22 José Esteban Muñoz has argued in *Cruising Utopia* that Giorno's recollection is a "picture of utopian transport and a reconfiguration of the social, a reimaging of our actual conditions of possibility, all of this in the face of a global epidemic" (38). Using Bloch and Adorno, Muñoz's reading of Giorno expertly communicates a mode of freedom and the urban possibility of transport. Giorno's text is a historical recollection of bliss that works dialectically with the contemporary political reality of HIV.
23 Giorno, *You Got to Burn*, 74.
24 Berman, *All That Is Solid Melts*, 155.
25 Berman, *All That Is Solid Melts*, 159.
26 Giorno, *You Got to Burn*, 74.
27 Giorno, *You Got to Burn*, 75–76.
28 Delany, *Motion of Light*, 201.
29 Delany, *Motion of Light*, 292.
30 Muñoz, "Future in the Present," 93–108.
31 Moten, *In the Break*, 158.
32 Barthes, *Lover's Discourse*, 40.

33 Haring, *Keith Haring Journals* (1996), 69–70.

34 Barthes, *Lover's Discourse*, 129.

2. "Trade" Marks

1 John Gruen, *Keith Haring*, 80.

2 Castleman, *Getting Up*, 26.

3 Woubshet, *Calendar of Loss*, 90.

4 Geldzahler, introduction to *Art in Transit*, n.p.

5 Geldzahler, introduction to *Art in Transit*, n.p.

6 Geldzahler, introduction to *Art in Transit*, n.p.

7 For a detailed history of graffiti in the New York City transit see Castleman, *Getting Up*, and Austin, *Taking the Train*.

8 Chauncey, *Gay New York*, 69–70.

9 Dynes, *Homolexis*, 140–41.

10 Hiram Pérez traces the history of trade within a modern literary tradition. His necessary intervention asks the question, "What is the relationship of trade to *trade*—that is the relation of international commerce to the proliferation of homosexual trade: rough trade, tearoom trade, military trade, and [citing the same configuration as Dynes] tomorrow's competition (née today's trade)?"; *Taste for Brown Bodies*, 2. His book also looks to technologies of racialization within fields of desire that are conditioned by class and fantasies of the primitive through an attentiveness to the work of Herman Melville. He does an extensive reading of Melville's *Billy Budd* through an attentiveness to the trade configuration.

11 Delany, *Times Square Red*, 12.

12 The details of DiCorcia's process are discussed by Peter Galassi in "Contemporaries: Philip-Lorca diCorcia," in Galassi, *Philip-Lorca DiCorcia*.

13 Delany, *Times Square Red*, 34.

14 Delany, *Times Square Red*, 46.

15 Delany, *Times Square Red*, 58.

16 Sennett, "New York Reflections," 20–21.

17 Sennett, "New York Reflections," 15.

18 Quoted in Sennett, "New York Reflections," 14–15.

19 Sidney Janis Gallery, *Post-Graffiti*, 9. Sennett slightly misquotes Haring's words when he cites this passage, substituting "LA II's imagination" (20–21) for Haring's "his [i.e., the image-maker's] imagination"—an error that underlines the universalizing frame of this approach to graffiti.

20 Dieckmann, "Tag Team," 114.

21 Dieckmann, "Tag Team," 115.

22 Moynihan, "Keith Haring's Silent Partner," 49.

23 Negrón-Muntaner, *Boricua Pop*, 129.

24 Negrón-Muntaner, *Boricua Pop*, 129.

25 John Gruen, *Keith Haring*, 138–39.

26 Julia Gruen, "Haring All Over."

1 Jones, "I'm Not Perfect."

2 John Gruen, *Keith Haring*, 142.

3 Thompson, "Requiem for the Degas," 138.

4 Kershaw, "Postcolonialism and Androgyny," 23.

5 Working from an essay by John Berger in which he discusses the modern establishment of the zoo, Chow states that the ethnic subject within capitalist liberalism assumes a position similar to that of the animal in a zoo: the premise of a natural habitat and human care for the animals' continued existence is a theater of civic marginalization. The animal on display exists for the spectator's gaze on the condition of its confinement, while becoming dependent on the care of the institution for its survival. Chow argues that this mode of apprehension is an apt metaphor for the marginalized ethnic subject. It is certainly possible to conceive Grace Jones's visibility in terms of socialization through and against whiteness—a socialization that takes shape both biographically (in the form of her intimate relations with white men) and artistically. See Chow, *Protestant Ethnic*, 95–97.

6 See Deleuze and Guattari, *Thousand Plateaus*, 3–4. I have also been influenced by Deleuze's theorization of immanence as a performative dimension opposed to that of transcendence. Deleuze's sketch of the opposition ("When you invoke something transcendent, you arrest movement, introducing interpretations instead of experimenting") speaks to my sense of Jones's refusal of definitive interpretation in the performance of movement. See Deleuze, *Negotiations*, 146.

7 Von Praunheim, *Army of Lovers*.

8 Jones, *I'll Never*, 123.

9 C. Carr describes this project in her stunning and harrowing biography of Haring's contemporary David Wojnarowicz, *Fire in the Belly*, 166.

10 Jones, *I'll Never*, 148.

11 Lawrence, *Loves Saves the Day*, and *Life and Death*.

12 Goude, *Jungle Fever*, 102.

13 Goude, *Jungle Fever*, 103.

14 Goude, *Jungle Fever*, 105.

15 Goude, *Jungle Fever*, 105.

16 Goude, *Jungle Fever*, 106.

17 Goude, *Jungle Fever*, 105.

18 Goude, *Jungle Fever*, 107.

19 Jones, *I'll Never*, 203.

20 Jones, *I'll Never*, 106.

21 Jones, *I'll Never*, 132.

22 Jones, *I'll Never*, 204.

23 John Gruen, *Keith Haring*, 116.

24 John Gruen, *Keith Haring*, 116.

25 Jones, *I'll Never*, 206–7.

26 John Gruen, *Keith Haring*, 118.

27 John Gruen, *Keith Haring*, 89.

28   Jones, *I'll Never*, 157.

29   Jones, *I'll Never*, 208.

30   Thompson, "Requiem for the Degas," 138.

31   Thompson, "Haring and the Dance," 214.

32   McMillan, "Introduction," 12.

33   Stephens, *Skin Acts*, 84.

34   Jones, *I'll Never*, 213.

4. Drips, Rust, and Residue

1   Haring, *Keith Haring Journals* (1996), 235.

2   Haring, *Keith Haring Journals* (1996), 236.

3   Haring, *Keith Haring Journals* (1996), 235.

4   Haring, *Keith Haring Journals* (1996), 236.

5   Muñoz, "Ephemera as Evidence," 7.

6   Benitez and Jackson, "From the Editors," 12.

7   Detrick, "'Kids,' Then and Now," D7.

8   Detrick, "'Kids,' Then and Now," D7.

9   Haring, preface to *Art in Transit*, n.p.

10   Haring, *Keith Haring Journals* (1996), 124–25.

11   Havadtoy, catalog statement.

12   Kerr, "History of Erasing Black Artists."

13   See Hilferty's 1991 documentary *Stop the Church* for an engrossing record of ACT UP's die-in at St. Patrick's Cathedral in New York City to protest Cardinal John O' Connor's irresponsible statements about condom use.

14   The SoHo shop closed in 2005. Haring also opened a Tokyo Pop Shop, which closed in 1988.

15   Grayson, "Bowery Flash," 27.

16   Reproductions of pages of the sketchbooks are available in Grayson, *Rosson Crow*.

17   Roland Barthes's classic distinction between the punctum and studium is elaborated in *Camera Lucida*.

18   Flusser, *Gestures*, 84.

19   Flusser, *Gestures*, 85.

20   Barthes, "That Old Thing, Art," 371.

Bibliography

Austin, Joe. *Taking the Train: How Graffiti Art Became an Urban Crisis in New York City*. New York: Columbia University Press, 2001.

Barthes, Roland. *Camera Lucida*. Translated by Richard Howard. New York: Hill and Wang, 1981.

Barthes, Roland. *A Lover's Discourse: Fragments*. Translated by Richard Howard. New York: Hill and Wang, 1978.

Barthes, Roland. "That Old Thing, Art . . ." Translated by Richard Howard. In *Pop Art: A Critical History*, edited by Steven Henry Madoff, 370–74. Berkeley: University of California Press, 1997.

Benitez, Abi, and Tom Jackson. "From the Editors." *Gayletter*, issue 5, 2016, 12.

Berman, Marshall. *All That Is Solid Melts into Air: The Experience of Modernity*. New York: Simon and Schuster, 1982.

Boyd, Gerald M. "Reagan Urges Abstinence for Young to Avoid AIDS." *New York Times*, April 2, 1987, A13.

Browning, Barbara. *Infectious Rhythm: Metaphors of Contagion and the Spread of African Culture*. New York: Routledge, 1998.

Carr, C. *Fire in the Belly: The Life and Times of David Wojnarowicz*. New York: Bloomsbury, 2012.

Castleman, Craig. *Getting Up: Subway Graffiti in New York*. Cambridge, MA: MIT Press, 1982.

Chauncey, George. *Gay New York: Gender, Urban Culture, and the Making of the Gay Male World, 1890–1940*. New York: Basic Books, 1995.

Chow, Rey. *The Protestant Ethnic and the Spirit of Capitalism*. New York: Columbia University Press, 2002.

Crimp, Douglas. *Melancholia and Moralism: Essays on AIDS and Queer Politics*. Cambridge, MA: MIT Press, 2002.

Cruz-Malavé, Arnaldo. *Queer Latino Testimonio, Keith Haring, and Juanito Xtravaganza*. New York: Palgrave Macmillan, 2007.

Cvetkovich, Ann. *An Archive of Feelings: Trauma, Sexuality, and Lesbian Public Culture*. Durham, NC: Duke University Press, 2003.

Delany, Samuel. *The Motion of Light in Water: Sex and Science Fiction Writing in the East Village*. New York: InsightOut Books, 2004.

Delany, Samuel. *Times Square Red/Times Square Blue*. New York: New York University Press, 2001.

Deleuze, Gilles. *Negotiations*. Translated by Martin Joughin. New York: Columbia University Press, 1995.

Deleuze, Gilles, and Félix Guattari. *A Thousand Plateaus*. Translated by Brian Massumi. Minneapolis: University of Minnesota Press, 1987.

Detrick, Ben. "'Kids,' Then and Now." *New York Times*, July 21, 2015, D7.

Dieckmann, Katherine. "Tag Team: LA 11 Remembers the Guy Who 'Draws Babies on the Door.'" *Village Voice*, May 15, 1990.

Dinshaw, Carolyn. *Getting Medieval: Sexualities and Communities, Pre- and Postmodern*. Durham, NC: Duke University Press, 1999.

Doyle, Jennifer. *Hold It against Me: Difficulty and Emotion in Contemporary Art*. Durham, NC: Duke University Press, 2013.

Dynes, Wayne. *Homolexis: A Historical and Cultural Lexicon of Homosexuality*. New York: Gay Academic Union, 1985.

Flusser, Vilém. *Gestures*. Translated by Nancy Ann Roth. Minneapolis: University of Minnesota Press, 2014.

Freeman, Elizabeth. *Time Binds: Queer Temporalities, Queer Histories*. Durham, NC: Duke University Press, 2010.

Fusco, Coco. "The Other History of Intercultural Performance." *Drama Review* 38, no. 1 (Spring 1994): 143–67.

Galassi, Peter. *Philip-Lorca DiCorcia*. New York: Museum of Modern Art, 2000.

Ganis, William V. *Andy Warhol's Serial Photography*. Cambridge, MA: MIT Press, 2004.

Geldzahler, Henry. Introduction to *Art in Transit: Subway Drawings*, by Keith Haring and Tseng Kwong Chi, n.p. New York: Harmony Books, 1984.

Genet, Jean. *Fragments of the Artwork*. Translated by Charlotte Mandell. Stanford, CA: Stanford University Press, 2003.

Giorno, John. *You Got to Burn to Shine: New and Selected Writings*. New York: High Risk Books, 1994.

González, Jennifer A. *Subject to Display: Reframing Race in Contemporary Installation Art*. Cambridge, MA: MIT Press, 2008.

Goude, Jean-Paul. *Jungle Fever*. Edited by Harold Hayes. New York: Xavier Moreau, 1981.

Grayson, Kathy. "Bowery Flash." In *Rosson Crow: Bowery Boys*, 27. New York: Deitch Projects, 2010.

Grayson, Kathy. *Rosson Crow: Bowery Boys*. New York: Deitch Projects, 2010.

Gruen, John. *Keith Haring: The Authorized Biography*. New York: Fireside, 1991.

Gruen, Julia. "Haring All Over." The Keith Haring Foundation website, November 1999. http://www.haring.com/!/selected_writing /haring-all-over#.WzgR 1n4hoWo.

Gysin, Brion. "The Sculpted Line." In *Back in No Time: The Brion Gysin Reader,* edited by Jason Weiss, 291. Middletown, CT: Wesleyan University Press, 2001.

Haring, Keith. *Keith Haring Journals.* New York: Viking, 1996.

Haring, Keith. *Keith Haring Journals.* New York: Penguin Classics, 2010.

Haring, Keith. Preface to *Art in Transit: Subway Drawings,* by Keith Haring and Tseng Kwong Chi, n.p. New York: Harmony Books, 1984.

Havadtoy, Sam. Statement in *Keith Haring Bronzes* catalog. New York: Gallery 56, 1990.

Hilferty, Robert, dir. *Stop the Church.* San Francisco: Frameline, 1991.

Jones, Grace. "I'm Not Perfect (But I'm Perfect for You)." Directed by Grace Jones. Music video, 3:52, 1986. https://www.youtube.com/watch?v=EMypXV1YJfw.

Jones, Grace, with Paul Morley. *I'll Never Write My Memoirs.* New York: Simon and Schuster, 2015.

Keith Haring: Retrospective. Whitney Museum of American Art, New York, June 18–September 21, 1997.

Kerr, Ted. "A History of Erasing Black Artists and Bodies from the AIDS Conversation." *Hyperallergic,* December 31, 2015. https://hyperallergic.com/264934/a-history-of-erasing-black-artists-and-bodies-from-the-aids-conversation/.

Kershaw, Miriam. "Postcolonialism and Androgyny: The Performance Art of Grace Jones." *Art Journal* 56, no. 4 (Winter 1997): 19–25.

Lawrence, Tim. *Life and Death on the New York Dance Floor, 1980–1983.* Durham, NC: Duke University Press, 2016.

Lawrence, Tim. *Love Saves the Day: A History of American Dance Music Culture, 1970–1979.* Durham, NC: Duke University Press, 2003.

Marcus, George E. "The Uses of Complicity in the Changing Mise-en-Scène of Anthropological Fieldwork." *Representations* 59 (Summer 1997): 85–108.

McMillan, Uri. "Introduction: Skin, Surface, Sensorium." *Women and Performance* 28, no. 1 (February 2018): 1–15.

Mercer, Kobena. *Welcome to the Jungle: New Positions in Black Cultural Studies.* New York: Routledge, 1994.

Miller, D. A. *Bringing Out Roland Barthes.* Berkeley: University of California Press, 1992.

Moten, Fred. *In the Break: The Aesthetics of the Black Radical Tradition.* Minneapolis: University of Minnesota Press, 2003.

Moynihan, Colin. "Keith Haring's Silent Partner." *Village Voice,* July 30, 2002, 49.

Muñoz, José Esteban. *Cruising Utopia: The Then and There of Queer Futurity.* New York: New York University Press, 2009.

Muñoz, José Esteban. "Ephemera as Evidence: Introductory Notes to Queer Acts." *Women and Performance: A Journal of Feminist Theory* 8, no. 2 (1996): 5–16.

Muñoz, José Esteban. "The Future in the Present: Sexual Avant-Gardes and the Performance of Utopia." In *The Futures of American Studies,* edited by Donald E. Pease and Robyn Wiegman, 93–108. Durham, NC: Duke University Press, 2002.

Musser, Amber Jamilla. *Sensational Flesh: Race, Power, and Masochism.* New York: New York University Press, 2014.

Negrón-Muntaner, Frances. *Boricua Pop: Puerto Ricans and the Latinization of American Culture*. New York: New York University Press, 2004.

Omi, Michael, and Howard Winant. *Racial Formation in the United States*. New York: Routledge, 1986.

Patton, Cindy. *Inventing AIDS*. New York: Routledge, 1990.

Pérez, Hiram. *A Taste for Brown Bodies: Gay Modernity and Cosmopolitan Desire*. New York: New York University Press, 2015.

Platow, Raphaela. *Keith Haring, 1978–1982*. Cincinnati, OH: Contemporary Arts Center, 2010.

Ricard, Rene. "The Radiant Child." *Artforum*, December 1981, 35–43.

Roth, Ronald C. "From Irony to the Apocalypse: The Evolution of Keith Haring's Social Critique." In *Keith Haring: Journey of the Radiant Baby*, edited by Rachel Arauz, 33–39. Piermont, NH: Bunker Hill, 2006.

Sennett, Richard. "New York Reflections." *Raritan* 10, no. 1 (Summer 1990): 20–21.

Sheff, David. "Keith Haring: Just Say Know." *Rolling Stone*, August 10, 1989, 59–66, 102.

Sidney Janis Gallery. *Post-Graffiti*. New York: Sidney Janis Gallery, 1983.

Stephens, Michelle. *Skin Acts: Race, Psychoanalysis, and the Black Male Performer*. Durham, NC: Duke University Press, 2014.

Taylor, Diana. "'You Are Here': The DNA of Performance." *Drama Review* 46, no. 1 (Spring 2002): 149–69.

Thompson, Robert Farris. "Haring and the Dance." In *Keith Haring*, edited by Elizabeth Sussman, 214–24. New York: Bulfinch, 1997.

Thompson, Robert Farris. "Requiem for the Degas of the B-Boys." *Artforum,* May 1990, 135–41.

van de Guchte, Maarten. "'Chance Favors the Prepared Mind': The Visual Anthropology of Keith Haring." In *Keith Haring: Future Primeval*, edited by Barry Blinderman, 80–89. New York: Abbeville, 1990.

von Praunheim, Rosa, dir. *An Army of Lovers, or, Revolt of the Perverts*. Berlin: von Praunheim, 1979.

Warhol, Andy. *The Andy Warhol Diaries*. Edited by Pat Hackett. New York: Warner Books, 1989.

Watney, Simon. *Policing Desire: Pornography, AIDS, and the Media*. 2nd ed. Minneapolis: University of Minnesota Press, 1997.

Woubshet, Dagmawi. *The Calendar of Loss: Sexuality and Mourning in the Early Era of AIDS*. Baltimore, MD: Johns Hopkins University Press, 2015.

Numbers in italics indicate illustrations.